THE Good LIFE

To my darling Michelle
and our three cheeky boys
Rex, Rudi and Roman.

And to my father, Jim:
we all miss you.

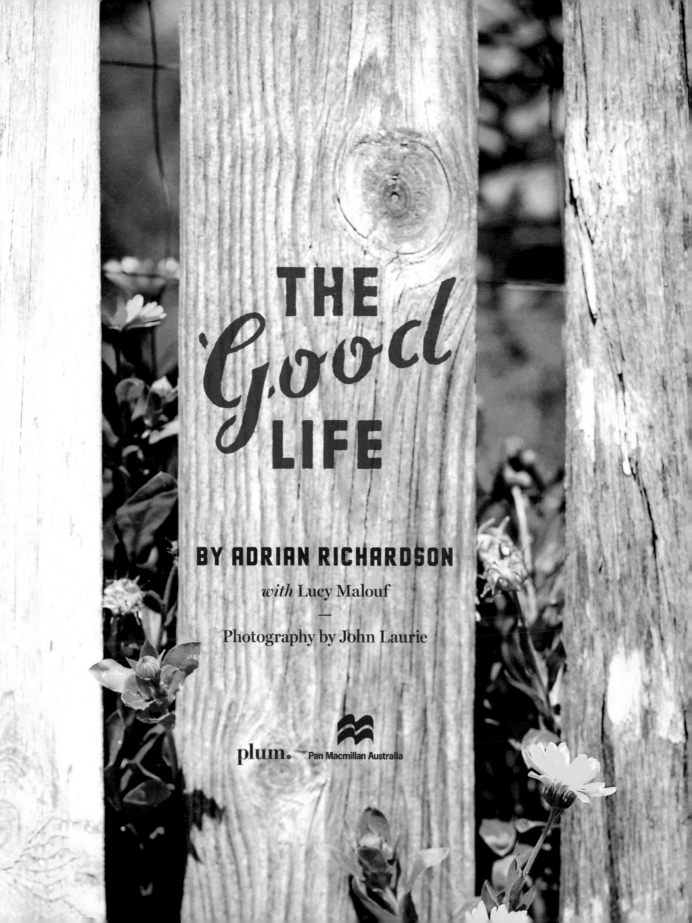

THE 'Good LIFE

BY ADRIAN RICHARDSON

with Lucy Malouf

—

Photography by John Laurie

plum. Pan Macmillan Australia

CONTENTS

Summer

INTRODUCTION

My most vivid childhood memories revolve around food in one way or another. As a boy, I loved to help my grandfather gather tomatoes and beans from the garden, help my mum pod peas, or to roll out pasta dough with my nonna to make her legendary ravioli. When my brother and I got home from school, the very first thing we'd do was rush to the kitchen for a few homemade biscotti. And there'd always be a pot bubbling away on the stove, the delicious aromas giving us a clue to dinner.

My family has strong Italian roots, and it's no secret how important food is to Italians. For us, food is what holds families together. It's the thing around which all traditions and celebrations revolve.

My three boys are all still little, so there's nothing they like more than hanging out with me and their mum and doing stuff together. And here's the great thing about food — whether it's growing, preparing, cooking or eating it, kids love getting involved!

I want my children to understand that carrots grow in the ground; to know that bacon comes from a pig, not a packet; that the pasta al forno they love so much doesn't come from a factory, but has been lovingly cooked by me or their mum. Even my youngest son helps out in the kitchen at dinnertime. It might mean that things take longer to get ready, and it's certainly not as peaceful as when they're plonked down in front of the telly, but I know that we all have more fun sharing the time together.

This book is not about flash, fancy, show-off food. Tricky, complicated meals are not really my style. It's about cooking and eating well with friends and family; getting back to basics and making things from scratch. Many of the recipes have sprung from my childhood, they are

dishes you can put together easily and which I hope you will automatically feel at home with. They are about comfort and simple pleasures. And, above all, they are about flavour.

It's easy to become disconnected from the natural rhythms of the year. We live in a world of abundance, where almost everything is available almost all the time. But just because it is possible to buy raspberries in the dead of winter, doesn't mean that you should. For a start, they won't taste all that good, and secondly, they'll be shockingly expensive. I know so many people bang on about buying seasonal produce, but even putting flavour aside, it's one of the best ways I know to help your budget.

My own family doesn't have a big backyard, but we have made the most of what we've got and have planted a vegie and herb patch. There's no better way to understand seasonality than planting, nurturing and harvesting your own vegies or herbs, so I really do encourage everyone to have a go — even if it's just a pot of parsley outside your back door. You can be creative with a small amount of space. I've even commandeered the nature strip outside my restaurant (with the local council's endorsement, of course), which provides us with herbs and salad leaves over the summer and bay leaves and rosemary all year round.

A spring lunch of grilled new-season asparagus with pesto and parmesan; Turkish-spiced kofte kebabs on a warm summer evening with a glass of homemade ginger beer, followed by a good old-fashioned strawberry sponge; then lamb shank and barley soup or my mum's roast chicken with parsley butter and cornbread stuffing as the nights begin to lengthen. These are the dishes I love to cook. Together they use the best ingredients at the right time of year, and I'm delighted to share them with you.

Vegetables

VEGETABLE TAGINE

SAUTÉED BROCCOLINI WITH GARLICKY, HERBY FRIED BREAD

MASH, MY WAY

BRUSSELS SPROUTS WITH BACON AND GARLIC BUTTER

NONNA'S ROMAN BEANS

CAULIFLOWER, CURRANTS AND PINE NUTS IN BROWN BUTTER

GRILLED ASPARAGUS WITH PESTO, PARMESAN AND
POACHED EGG

ROAST VEGETABLES WITH ROSEMARY, AND A
GARLIC AND FETA DRESSING

LETTUCE AND PEAS, FRENCH STYLE

BAKED ZUCCHINI WITH A TANGY SOURDOUGH STUFFING

CAULIFLOWER AND CARROT CURRY

NONNA'S MELANZANE PIZZAIOLA

ALMOST THE FIRST thing my wife Michelle and I did after moving into our new home recently was to work out where to plant the vegie patch. We then spent a Sunday afternoon digging away, with the kids dropping seeds into the soil, and I remembered my brother and I doing the exact same thing with my nonno and nonna in their back garden when we were kids.

I guess it's a cliché that Italians love to grow their own vegetables, but I remember how proud my grandparents were of their garden. And our family seemed to have a steady supply of produce all year round: lemons from the tree and grapes from the vine, and the best, tastiest tomatoes, green beans, plump purple eggplants and sweet carrots, and potatoes and silverbeet long into winter.

These days I think more and more of us are wanting to grow things for ourselves. Partly it makes you take time out from the hustle and bustle of daily life, but the rewards also give you so much pleasure. I'm not talking about serious self-sufficiency, either. A small patch or pot planted with a few zucchini or lettuces will be suprisingly productive. And as a bonus, it's a great way to get the kids to eat more vegies as they always seem keener to eat stuff they've grown themselves.

If you don't have the opportunity to get your hands into the earth, then I recommend farmers' markets as a great place to shop for the best seasonal produce. You'll soon discover how much better it tastes than the stuff you buy in supermarkets, which has often been transported thousands of kilometres and is far from fresh.

In this chapter you will find some of my favourite vegie side dishes, but also some great recipes that serve as a main meal — as I reckon vegetables are long overdue to have their turn as the hero at the dinner table.

VEGETABLE TAGINE

Tagines get their name from a type of earthenware cooking pot used in North Africa to prepare beautifully tender, slow-cooked dishes. Tagines do take time to prepare but the rewards are well worth the effort. Serve with steamed couscous and Minted Yoghurt (page 120).

Preheat the oven to 160°C.

To make the broth, heat the butter and oil in a large heavy-based saucepan. Add the onion and garlic and fry gently for 3–4 minutes, until the onion is soft but not coloured. Add the chilli and spices and cook for 2–3 minutes, stirring. It should be fantastically aromatic. Add the tomato passata, water and salt and bring to a boil. Lower the heat and simmer for 4–5 minutes, then remove from the heat.

Arrange the vegetables except the zucchini and beans, and the dates, in a casserole pot. Pour on the hot broth, then cover and bake for 30 minutes. Add the zucchini and beans and bake for a further 30 minutes, or until the vegetables are tender.

To serve, sprinkle on the coriander and lemon juice.

Serves 4

1 onion, cut into wedges

2 large carrots, peeled and thickly sliced

1 large potato, peeled and thickly sliced

1 parsnip, peeled and cut into chunks

150 g swede, peeled and thickly sliced

150 g pumpkin, skinned, seeded and cut into 2 cm dice

200 g zucchini, cut into chunks

200 g green beans, sliced

180 g fresh dates

1 cup roughly chopped coriander leaves

juice of 1 lemon

Broth

2 tablespoons butter

2 tablespoons olive oil

2 onions, finely diced

5 garlic cloves, crushed

1 teaspoon chopped fresh chilli

1 tablespoon cumin seeds, toasted and ground

1 tablespoon coriander seeds, toasted and ground

1 teaspoon caraway seeds

1 teaspoon ground cinnamon

1 teaspoon ground allspice

1 teaspoon ground turmeric

1 tablespoon ground ginger

1 large pinch of saffron threads

2 cardamom pods, cracked

750 ml Tomato Passata (for recipe see page 156)

500 ml water

salt

SAUTÉED BROCCOLINI WITH GARLICKY, HERBY FRIED BREAD

The great thing about broccolini is that it is completely edible, which cuts down on the preparation time. This recipe works just as well with broccoli rabe, chinese broccoli and ordinary broccoli — and even with green beans.

Bring a large saucepan of salted water to a boil. Add the broccolini, return to the boil, then simmer for 2–3 minutes or until just tender. Tip into a colander to drain then place on a clean tea towel to dry.

Heat 60 ml of the oil in a large heavy-based frying pan. Add the bread and fry over medium heat for 3–4 minutes or until crisp and golden. Add the garlic and fry for 2 minutes, adding another splash of oil to the pan if necessary. Add the herbs and season with salt and pepper. Fry for another 30 seconds then transfer to a warm dish.

Add the rest of the oil to the pan and fry the broccolini for 2–3 minutes, tossing gently. Arrange on a warm serving platter and scatter the fried bread on top.

Serves 4 as a side dish

1 bunch (approximately 400 g) broccolini

75 ml olive oil

3 thick slices of sourdough bread, crusts removed and cut into 1 cm cubes

4 garlic cloves, crushed

3 tablespoons chopped flat-leaf parsley

2 tablespoons chopped thyme

1 tablespoon dried oregano

salt

freshly ground black pepper

MASH, MY WAY

However you make it, I reckon it's hard to go wrong with mash — as long as you don't forget the cream and butter! There has to be some joy in life, after all. When I make my mash, I peel and boil the potatoes whole as I find dicing them makes them absorb too much water.

Peel the potatoes and put them in a large saucepan of cold, salted water. Bring to a boil, then lower the heat and simmer until tender. This will take up to 50 minutes, depending on the size of the potatoes. When the potatoes are cooked, tip them into a colander to drain.

Add the cream and butter to the hot saucepan. Push the hot potatoes through a potato ricer or food mill straight onto the cream and butter. Beat with a spoon, then season to taste.

Serves 4 as a side dish

750 g nicola potatoes (or another yellow, waxy variety)

150 ml cream (or more to taste)

150 g butter (or more to taste)

salt

freshly ground black pepper

BRUSSELS SPROUTS WITH BACON AND GARLIC BUTTER

When it comes to brussels sprouts, you either love 'em or hate 'em; I don't think there is anything in between. But if you are in the hate 'em camp, then this recipe might just win you over.

Bring a large saucepan of salted water to a boil. Remove the outer leaves from the brussels sprouts, trim off the bases and cut them in half. Add to the pan and allow the water to return to the boil, then simmer for 2–3 minutes or until just tender. Tip into a colander to drain.

Heat the oil in a large heavy-based frying pan. Add the onion and garlic and fry over medium heat for 5 minutes, or until soft and beginning to colour. Add the bacon and fry for 3–4 minutes until starting to crisp.

Add the brussels sprouts and butter to the pan. Season to taste and mix everything together well. Stir in the parsley and serve.

Serves 4 as a side dish

400 g brussels sprouts

2 tablespoons olive oil

$\frac{1}{2}$ medium onion, finely diced

4 garlic cloves, crushed

2 thick-cut bacon rashers, rinds removed, finely sliced

large knob of butter

salt

freshly ground black pepper

3 tablespoons roughly chopped flat-leaf parsley

NONNA'S ROMAN BEANS

Roman or runner beans are wide, flat beans that are a little paler in colour than regular green beans. They are beautiful when cooked until very soft and tender.

This is one of my nonna's recipes, which she made all the time using beans from her garden. It's a dish that can be eaten hot, warm or cold, or best of all, spooned between two slices of thickly buttered bread. And it's the one dish that I always serve with good Italian sausages (page 264).

Trim the beans and, if they are very big, cut them in half on the diagonal.

Heat the oil in a large heavy-based saucepan. Add the onion and garlic and fry gently for 3–4 minutes, until the onion is soft but not coloured. Add the beans, tomato passata and basil and season with salt and pepper. Bring to a boil then lower the heat and simmer, covered, for 20–30 minutes until the beans are soft and almost falling apart in the sauce.

Remove from the heat and stir in the lemon juice and parsley. Serve either hot from the pan, or warm, or cold.

Serves 4 as a side dish

500 g Roman beans

3 tablespoons extra-virgin olive oil

1 medium onion, finely diced

2 garlic cloves, sliced

250 ml Tomato Passata (for recipe see page 156), or 400 g ripe tomatoes, peeled, seeded and chopped

6 basil leaves

salt

freshly ground black pepper

squeeze of lemon juice

2 tablespoons chopped flat-leaf parsley

CAULIFLOWER, CURRANTS AND PINE NUTS IN BROWN BUTTER

This is a rather unusual and very tasty side dish, and a great way to get the kids to eat cauliflower.

Put the cauliflower into a large saucepan with plenty of cold water. Bring to a boil, then add 1 teaspoon of salt and lower the heat. Simmer for 5 minutes, or until the cauliflower is just tender. Tip into a colander to drain.

Heat the butter in a large frying pan until it turns nutty brown. Add the cauliflower and sauté for 3–4 minutes, or until it begins to colour a lovely golden brown. Remove the pan from the heat and stir in the currants, pine nuts and parsley. Season to taste, add the lemon juice and serve straight away.

Serves 6–8 as a side dish

1 kg cauliflower, broken into bite-sized florets

salt

150 g butter

100 g currants

100 g pine nuts

$\frac{1}{2}$ cup chopped flat-leaf parsley

freshly ground black pepper

juice of $\frac{1}{2}$ lemon

GRILLED ASPARAGUS WITH PESTO, PARMESAN AND POACHED EGG

There are a few different types of asparagus around these days — thick and thin, green and white, and even wild asparagus! But I think the most important thing is to eat it when it's in season in spring and summer. The expensive stuff that you get out of season will have been transported a long way to get to the shelves, so it won't be nearly as fresh or delicious. I reckon it's far better to eat loads of it when there's plenty around, and then just be patient until next season.

This is a simple but brilliantly tasty way to serve asparagus. You can serve it as a side dish or as a stunning little starter for a dinner party, or as a vegetarian alternative at a barbecue.

Preheat your barbecue or a griddle pan to medium.

To prepare the asparagus, simply bend them at the base of each spear until they snap. They should break where the tender green part begins to get woody and tough. Discard the woody ends and put the asparagus in a large mixing bowl. Drizzle on half of the oil and season with salt and pepper, then use your hands to toss the asparagus around until evenly coated.

Bring a large saucepan of water to a gentle boil and add the vinegar. Poach the eggs, one at a time, for 3 minutes, or until the white is completely set. Use a slotted spoon to transfer them to a bowl of iced water, which stops them cooking further, then lift onto a clean tea towel. The eggs can be poached to this stage ahead of time.

Place the asparagus on the barbecue or griddle and cook on all sides until the spears soften and become nice and charred. As soon as they are cooked, put them back in the mixing bowl and toss with the remaining oil and pesto.

Reheat the eggs in a pan of gently simmering water for 30–60 seconds.

Divide the asparagus between 4 plates and top with the eggs and parmesan.

Serves 4 as a side dish

400 g thick asparagus
2 tablespoons extra-virgin olive oil
salt
freshly ground black pepper
1 teaspoon white vinegar
4 eggs
125 ml Pesto (for recipe see page 27)
shavings of parmesan to serve

ROAST VEGETABLES WITH ROSEMARY, AND A GARLIC AND FETA DRESSING

Root vegetables are great for roasting as it intensifies their natural sugars. This is a very versatile dish as you can serve it hot from the oven or at room temperature as a salad.

Preheat the oven to 200°C.

Arrange the vegetables on a large roasting tray. Try to keep each vegetable in a separate part of the tray as they will cook at different rates, and that way you can easily remove those that cook early if they are becoming too brown. Drizzle the vegetables with the oil and season generously with salt and pepper. Cook for 15–20 minutes, or until the vegetables are golden brown and tender but not disintegrating, removing any vegetables as needed.

While the vegetables are roasting, prepare the dressing. Blitz the garlic and lemon juice in a food processor, then add the feta and blend until smooth. With the motor running, slowly drizzle in the oil until well combined. Season with pepper and taste, adding salt if necessary (the feta is already salty).

Transfer the roasted vegetables to a warm serving platter and scatter on the rosemary. Drizzle on the dressing, scatter on the parsley and serve straight away. Or, if you want to serve this as a salad at room temperature, dress the vegetables while still warm, reserving a small amount of dressing, and leave to cool. Drizzle with the remaining dressing just before serving.

Serves 4–6

2 large potatoes, peeled and cut into large wedges

2 large carrots, peeled and cut lengthwise into strips

2 sweet potatoes, peeled and cut into rounds

1 large beetroot, peeled and cut into 2 cm wedges

1 large celeriac, peeled and cut into 2 cm wedges

1 red onion, cut into wedges

3 tablespoons olive oil

salt

freshly ground black pepper

sprig of rosemary, leaves picked and roughly chopped

½ cup finely chopped flat-leaf parsley

Dressing

2 garlic cloves

juice of 2 lemons

100 g feta, roughly crumbled

3 tablespoons extra-virgin olive oil

½ teaspoon freshly ground white pepper

LETTUCE AND PEAS, FRENCH-STYLE

I was introduced to this dish by a friend of mine who is a French chef. I don't usually like cooked lettuce, but as I discovered, when it's combined with peas, bacon and heaps of butter, it is delicious.

Melt the butter in a small saucepan. Add the shallots, garlic and bacon and fry over gentle heat for 5–10 minutes until very soft, but not brown.

Add the peas and stock and bring to a boil. Lower the heat and simmer for 4–5 minutes, or until the peas are barely tender. Add the lettuce and simmer for 5 minutes, or until the peas and lettuce are both cooked and the liquid has reduced to a nice sauce — it shouldn't be too liquid. Stir in the parsley and serve.

Serves 4 as a side dish

150 g butter

2 shallots, finely diced

1 garlic clove, crushed

1 thick-cut bacon rasher, rind removed, finely diced

400 g freshly podded peas

250 ml chicken stock

$\frac{1}{4}$ iceberg lettuce, finely shredded

3 tablespoons chopped flat-leaf parsley

BAKED ZUCCHINI WITH A TANGY SOURDOUGH STUFFING

By late spring there are plenty of large zucchini around — and they are perfect for stuffing. This dish is really easy to make and is great for doubling to feed a crowd. If you like, add minced pork or bacon to the stuffing; just fry it up with the onion and garlic. Although fresh capsicum is fine, for an extra depth of flavour I like to roast the capsicum before adding it to the stuffing (you can also buy roasted capsicum marinated in oil from good delicatessens).

Preheat the oven to 180°C. Slice the zucchini along their length and use a teaspoon to scoop out the seedy centre.

Melt the butter in a large heavy-based frying pan. Add the onion and garlic and fry gently for 3–4 minutes, until the onion is soft but not coloured. Add the olives, capsicum, herbs, lemon zest and breadcrumbs and stir until well combined. Remove from the heat and season with salt and pepper.

Arrange the 4 zucchini halves in a small oven tray just large enough to contain them. You may need to slice a thin layer from the base so they can sit flat. Fill each zucchini with a generous amount of the breadcrumb stuffing. Top with grated pecorino or parmesan and bake for 25 minutes, or until the zucchini are soft and the stuffing is golden brown.

Serves 4

2 large zucchini

100 g butter

1 onion, finely diced

2 garlic cloves, crushed

50 g green olives, pitted and roughly chopped

1 red capsicum, roasted, peeled, seeded and roughly chopped

3 tablespoons roughly chopped flat-leaf parsley

1 teaspoon dried oregano

grated zest of 1 lemon

100 g sourdough breadcrumbs

salt

freshly ground black pepper

$\frac{1}{4}$ cup pecorino or parmesan, freshly grated

CAULIFLOWER AND CARROT CURRY

Some curries can be quite high in saturated fat because they use a lot of meat and coconut cream. This vegetable curry is fresh-tasting and healthy, and everyone seems to love it. It's pretty quick and easy to make, but I do think it's important to use a good-quality curry powder or curry paste. Then, the addition of a few extra spices really improves the flavour. As with most curries, this one is even better if you serve it the day after you make it, as the flavours have more time to develop.

Heat the oil in a large heavy-based saucepan. Add the onion and garlic and fry gently for 3–4 minutes, until the onion is soft but not coloured. Add the ginger, chilli (if using) and coriander and cook for 2–3 minutes, stirring well. Now stir in the curry powder or paste, spices and bay leaf.

Add the grated carrot, raisins, tomato passata and water and bring to a boil. Lower the heat and simmer for 2 minutes. Add the sliced carrots and cauliflower and simmer uncovered for 30–40 minutes, until the vegetables are tender. Season with salt and pepper and serve with steamed rice and lots of creamy yoghurt.

Serves 4

3 tablespoons vegetable oil

1 onion, finely diced

3 garlic cloves, crushed

1 tablespoon grated ginger

1 small red chilli, roughly chopped (optional)

$\frac{1}{2}$ cup roughly chopped coriander (stalks and leaves)

2 tablespoons good-quality curry powder or your favourite curry paste

1 tablespoon cumin seeds, toasted and ground

1 teaspoon caraway seeds, ground

1 teaspoon ground allspice

1 teaspoon mustard seeds

1 teaspoon freshly ground white pepper

1 bay leaf

4 large carrots, 2 grated and 2 sliced

45 g raisins

500 ml Tomato Passata (for recipe see page 156)

750 ml water

$\frac{1}{2}$ cauliflower, cut into large florets

salt

freshly ground black pepper

NONNA'S EGGPLANT PIZZAIOLA

If you can imagine a vegetarian lasagne without the layers of pasta — with slices of fried eggplant instead — then this is what it would look like. It's fantastic straight out of the oven, and just as good the next day straight out of the fridge!

I find it's a good idea to salt the eggplant overnight as it helps to draw out any bitterness.

Layer the eggplant slices in a tray, scattering generously with salt as you go. Cover with plastic wrap and weight with a chopping board. Put the tray in the refrigerator overnight to extract as much liquid from the eggplant as possible.

Rinse the eggplant in cold water and pat dry with paper towel.

Pour olive oil into a large heavy-based frying pan to a depth of 1 cm, and heat gently.

While the oil is heating, dust the eggplant slices in flour, then dip into the beaten egg. Shallow-fry the slices in batches for 2 minutes on each side, or until golden brown. Move the slices around in the hot oil to stop them sticking and burning. Once cooked, transfer to a wire rack to drain and season lightly with salt and pepper.

Preheat the oven to 160°C. Spread a little of the tomato passata over the base of a 20 cm baking dish. Arrange a layer of eggplant slices on top, then scatter with a few basil leaves, some olives, a few slices of bocconcini and some grated mozzarella. Continue layering until all the ingredients are used, finishing with a layer of cheese.

Cover with foil and bake for 30 minutes. Remove the foil and bake for a further 15–20 minutes until golden brown.

Serves 4

3 large eggplants, peeled and cut into 1 cm slices

salt

olive oil

plain flour

3 eggs, lightly beaten

freshly ground white pepper

500 ml Tomato Passata (for recipe see page 156)

$\frac{1}{2}$ cup basil leaves

$\frac{1}{4}$ cup green olives, pitted and roughly chopped

200 g bocconcini, finely sliced

100 g mozzarella, freshly grated

Herbs

I'm a huge fan of herbs. I use them in just about every meal as I think they are brilliant at bringing dishes to life.

You can use herbs in all kinds of ways. Soft-leafed herbs combine with other greenery in salads to add instant little flavour hits, or can be sprinkled over cooked dishes just before serving to release their wonderful aromas and add that last-minute freshness and vitality. The more robust, woody herbs are used from the beginning of the cooking process to infuse stocks, soups and stews with another layer and complexity of flavour.

I think the best way to enjoy herbs is to pick them when you need them from your own garden or window box. Most herbs are pretty resilient and, seriously, anyone can grow them on even the smallest balcony. All that most herbs need by way of nurturing is a bit of water, and time.

If you can't grow your own, then do try to buy fresh herbs from a greengrocer or a farmers' market. Wash them thoroughly and wrap them, still wet, in damp paper towel and a sheet of plastic wrap — or store them in an airtight container. They should last a good week in the fridge.

SALSA VERDE

This intensely flavoured sauce goes well with grilled fish and meat, or cold meats, or served as a pasta sauce as you would pesto.

150 g green olives, pitted and chopped

80 g gherkins, chopped

3 tablespoons chopped flat-leaf parsley

1 garlic clove, finely chopped (optional)

juice of 1 lemon

3 tablespoons extra-virgin olive oil

salt

freshly ground black pepper

Combine the olives, gherkins, parsley and garlic (if using) in a mixing bowl and add the lemon juice and oil. Stir well, then season to taste. Leave to sit for 30 minutes at room temperature so the flavours can develop. Stir briefly before serving.

Makes 250 ml

PESTO

Loads of people say that pesto is their favourite pasta sauce, and the homemade stuff is much tastier than any of the ready-made versions. Believe me — you'll really notice the difference in texture and flavour.

2 garlic cloves, crushed

½ teaspoon salt

150 ml olive oil

100 g pine nuts, toasted

3 cups well-packed basil leaves

75 g parmesan (grana padano or parmigiano reggiano are best), grated

freshly ground black pepper

Combine the garlic and salt with half the oil in a food processor and whiz to a smooth paste. Add half the pine nuts and pulse until blended. Add the basil and whiz to a coarse paste. Pulse in the remaining pine nuts, making sure there is still some texture. Tip into a mixing bowl and stir in the parmesan and the rest of the oil. Season to taste with extra salt and pepper and transfer to a jar. Cover the surface with a film of oil, which helps to prevent the pesto discolouring. Store in the refrigerator for up to 2 weeks, or freeze for up to 3 months.

Makes 400 ml

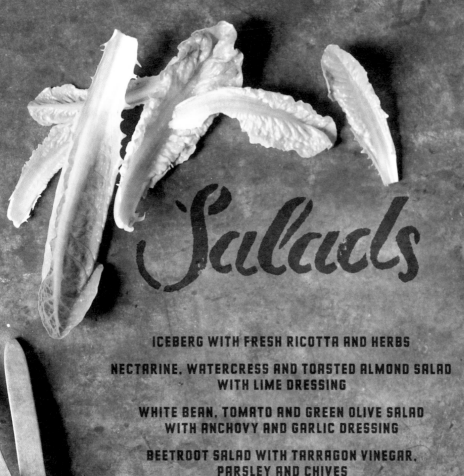

Salads

ICEBERG WITH FRESH RICOTTA AND HERBS

NECTARINE, WATERCRESS AND TOASTED ALMOND SALAD
WITH LIME DRESSING

WHITE BEAN, TOMATO AND GREEN OLIVE SALAD
WITH ANCHOVY AND GARLIC DRESSING

BEETROOT SALAD WITH TARRAGON VINEGAR,
PARSLEY AND CHIVES

SWEET FIG, PROSCIUTTO AND BURRATA SALAD
WITH CRUNCHY BREAD AND BALSAMIC DRESSING

TABBOULEH

ARTICHOKE, BRESAOLA AND TRUFFLED
PECORINO SALAD WITH POACHED EGGS

ASIAN-STYLE BUCKWHEAT
NOODLE SALAD

ICEBERG WITH FRESH RICOTTA AND HERBS

There are so many fancy lettuces around these days that it sometimes seems as if the good old iceberg lettuce has been left behind. I think it's time to bring it back, and this simple salad really shows off its lovely crispness. Serve the salad as an accompaniment or even as a refreshing starter on a warm spring day.

When choosing your lettuce, make sure you pick one that feels heavy for its size. The leaves should be tightly furled and there shouldn't be any that are slimy or brown.

Fresh ricotta is available from good delicatessens and Italian food stores. The one I buy is so fresh that it is sometimes still warm!

To make the dressing, whisk all the ingredients together and set aside until ready to use.

Remove the outer leaves from the lettuce. Wash the lettuce and dry it thoroughly, then cut it into quarters and tear it into bite-sized pieces. Arrange the lettuce on a serving platter and scatter on the ricotta, pine nuts and herbs. Drizzle on the dressing and serve straight away.

Serves 6

1 large iceberg lettuce

200 g fresh ricotta, roughly crumbled

3 tablespoons pine nuts, toasted

3 tablespoons chives snipped in 4 cm lengths

3 tablespoons roughly chopped flat-leaf parsley

3 tablespoons torn basil leaves

10 mint leaves, roughly torn

Dressing

3 tablespoons extra-virgin olive oil

3 tablespoons lemon juice

1 tablespoon French grain mustard

1 tablespoon chopped thyme

salt

freshly ground black pepper

NECTARINE, WATERCRESS AND TOASTED ALMOND SALAD WITH LIME DRESSING

Nectarines have a fairly short season, so when they are good I like to serve them in as many ways as I can, both sweet and savoury.

This simple, light salad goes brilliantly with crisp roasted duck or barbecued chicken. If I feel like making something a bit fancy, I sometimes add some roughly crumbled goat's cheese, too.

To make the dressing, whisk all the ingredients together and set aside until ready to use.

Cut the nectarines in half and remove the stones (there's no need to peel them). Slice each half into thirds and arrange on a large serving platter.

Use a small, sharp knife to cut the peel from the lime. Hold the lime in one hand and use the other hand to cut on either side of each segment to remove wedges of flesh, leaving the membranes behind.

Scatter the lime segments over the nectarines, followed by the watercress, herbs and almonds. Drizzle on the dressing and serve straight away.

Serves 4

6 ripe nectarines

1 lime

2 cups watercress sprigs

3 tablespoons flat-leaf parsley

3 tablespoons chives snipped in 4 cm lengths

3 tablespoons dill sprigs

3 tablespoons almonds, toasted and roughly chopped

Dressing

3 tablespoons extra-virgin olive oil

juice of 2 limes

1 teaspoon French grain mustard

salt

freshly ground black pepper

WHITE BEAN, TOMATO AND GREEN OLIVE SALAD WITH ANCHOVY AND GARLIC DRESSING

This robust salad is full of strong flavours and works well made with any dried white beans: lima, navy and cannellini beans, for instance, would all be ideal. You can use tinned beans if you like, but I think their flavour and texture are not as good as dried beans that you soak and simmer yourself.

To make the dressing, crush the garlic clove with the salt in a mortar. Whisk the garlic paste with the oil and vinegar, then gently whisk in the chopped anchovies. Season to taste with pepper and a little extra salt if needed (don't forget that the anchovies are salty). Set aside until ready to use.

To make the salad, heat the oil in a large heavy-based frying pan. Add the cubes of bread and fry over medium heat for 3–4 minutes, or until you have crisp, golden croutons. Tip onto paper towel to drain. Keep the croutons warm until ready to serve.

Combine the remaining ingredients in a large mixing bowl. Pour on enough dressing to moisten the salad and toss it together gently. Tip onto a serving platter and scatter on the warm croutons. Serve the extra dressing in a jug on the side so people can help themselves.

Serves 4

$2\frac{1}{2}$ tablespoons olive oil

3 slices of sourdough bread, crusts removed and cut into 2 cm cubes

400 g cooked white beans

4 roma tomatoes, roughly chopped

100 g green olives, pitted and roughly chopped

6 spring onions, sliced

1 cup flat-leaf parsley

1 cup basil leaves

Dressing

1 garlic clove

$\frac{1}{2}$ teaspoon salt

3 tablespoons extra-virgin olive oil

3 tablespoons white wine vinegar

4 large anchovy fillets, finely chopped

freshly ground black pepper

BEETROOT SALAD WITH TARRAGON VINEGAR, PARSLEY AND CHIVES

This salad is one of my favourites — tasty, healthy and easy to prepare. There is no comparing freshly cooked beetroot with the tinned stuff, and simmering beetroots with vinegar really brings out their earthy, sweet flavour. The first time you try this dish you'll see what I mean.

Put the beetroots in a large saucepan and add the vinegar, sugar and salt. Cover with cold water and bring to a boil. Lower the heat and simmer for 1–1½ hours, or until the beetroots are tender. Allow to cool in the liquid.

When completely cold, peel the beetroots and trim away any stalky bits. Cut into fairly small dice and place in a mixing bowl.

Whisk all the dressing ingredients together. Pour onto the beetroot and toss to combine. Taste and adjust the seasoning and serve straight away.

Serves 6

1 kg large beetroots, roots and tops trimmed

500 ml white vinegar

200 g sugar

2 tablespoons salt

Dressing

125 ml extra-virgin olive oil

3 tablespoons Tarragon Vinegar (page 43)

½ cup roughly chopped flat-leaf parsley

½ cup chives snipped in 1 cm lengths

salt

freshly ground black pepper

SWEET FIG, PROSCIUTTO AND BURRATA SALAD WITH CRUNCHY BREAD AND BALSAMIC DRESSING

Burrata is a fresh Italian cheese made from mozzarella and cream, and you can get cow's milk and buffalo milk varieties. It is made by hand and has a firm outer shell and a very soft, creamy centre. It comes in various sizes, but for this recipe I use ones that are just a bit smaller than a tennis ball. You can serve this as one big salad, or plate it up for a more formal first course.

To make the dressing, whisk all the ingredients together and set aside until ready to use.

Heat the oil in a large heavy-based frying pan. Add the cubes of bread and fry over medium heat for 3–4 minutes or until you have crisp, golden croutons. Tip onto paper towel to drain, then divide between 4 shallow bowls.

In a large mixing bowl, combine the lettuce leaves, herbs and prosciutto. Pour on enough dressing to moisten and toss gently.

To serve, place 1 burrata on top of the croutons in each bowl. Arrange 8 pieces of fig around each ball of cheese, then scatter the salad on top. Break the cheeses open to reveal their creamy centres, drizzle with a little more dressing and serve straight away.

Serves 4

3 tablespoons olive oil

4 thick slices of sourdough bread, crusts removed and cut into 2 cm cubes

2 cups mixed lettuce leaves

¼ cup chopped flat-leaf parsley

¼ cup chives snipped in 4 cm lengths

¼ cup basil leaves

8 slices of prosciutto, cut into 1 cm strips

4 burrata

8 ripe figs, quartered

Dressing

3 tablespoons extra-virgin olive oil

3 tablespoons good-quality balsamic vinegar

1 teaspoon caster sugar

salt

freshly ground black pepper

TABBOULEH

This is one of my all-time-favourite salads. It seems to go with so many things, from grills and barbecues to a Sunday roast lamb. Tabbouleh is traditionally made with burghul (cracked wheat), but I like to use couscous because it is so widely available these days. You can use leftover couscous, but it only takes a few minutes to soak and soften fresh couscous in a little boiling water.

Tabouleh is best made just before you are ready to serve it, or it runs the risk of going soggy.

Combine the couscous and boiling water in a small mixing bowl. Stir in 1 tablespoon of the oil and cover, leaving the couscous to cook and swell. Allow to cool then fluff up the grains with a fork.

Combine the cooled couscous with the remaining ingredients, including the remaining oil, in a large mixing bowl. Toss together gently but evenly. Taste and adjust the seasoning to your liking. Serve as soon as possible.

Serves 4

3 tablespoons couscous

3 tablespoons boiling water

80 ml extra-virgin olive oil

2 spring onions, finely sliced

2 roma tomatoes, seeded and finely diced

2 cups chopped flat-leaf parsley

3 tablespoons roughly chopped mint leaves

juice of 2 lemons

salt

freshly ground black pepper

ARTICHOKE, BRESAOLA AND TRUFFLED PECORINO SALAD WITH POACHED EGGS

You can buy artichokes preserved in oil from the deli counter in good supermarkets. They have an appealing, almost metallic flavour, which goes brilliantly with Italian bresaola (or other air-dried beef), and with sharp, salty pecorino. I particularly like pecorino that is infused with earthy truffles. Add a warm poached egg and you have a really amazing lunch dish or starter for a dinner party.

Pull the preserved artichokes apart and put them in a large mixing bowl with the watercress, witlof, radicchio, chives and pecorino.

Bring a large saucepan of water to a gentle boil and add the white vinegar. Crack one of the eggs into a cup, being careful not to break the yolk. Use a long spoon to stir the water in the pan to create a mini whirlpool. Carefully slip the egg into the water and allow the swirling water to shape it into a ball. Poach for 1–2 minutes, or until the white has set. Carefully remove the egg with a slotted spoon and place on a clean tea towel to drain while you poach the remaining eggs. The eggs can be poached to this stage ahead of time and cooled on ice. You can reheat them all together for 30–45 seconds in gently simmering water just before you serve them.

Arrange 5 slices of bresaola on each of 4 plates. Add 60 ml of the oil and all of the tarragon vinegar to the bowl of salad and season with salt and pepper. Toss gently, then divide the salad between the plates. Top each serve with a poached egg, drizzle with the remaining oil and serve immediately.

Serves 4

220 g artichoke hearts in oil, drained

2 cups loosely packed watercress sprigs

2 witlof, outer leaves discarded, leaves separated

2–3 radicchio leaves, torn

2 tablespoons snipped chives

50 g truffled pecorino, shaved

1 tablespoon white vinegar

4 eggs

20 slices Bresaola (page 202)

80 ml extra-virgin olive oil

2 tablespoons Tarragon Vinegar (page 43)

salt

freshly ground black pepper

ASIAN-STYLE BUCKWHEAT NOODLE SALAD

This Asian-inspired salad is a firm favourite in my family and I make it at home regularly, sometimes on its own or sometimes adding poached or grilled chicken. The buckwheat noodles have a lovely toasty, nutty flavour, and my boys just love slurping them up. These noodles along with deep-fried shallots are readily available from Asian supermarkets.

To make the dressing, whisk all the ingredients together and set aside until ready to use.

Cook the noodles in plenty of salted boiling water until tender. Tip into a colander and rinse under cold water for a few moments. Leave in the colander to drain and cool, tossing from time to time, then tip into a large mixing bowl. Add half of the dressing and toss to evenly coat the noodles, then divide between 4 shallow bowls.

Combine the remaining ingredients in the mixing bowl. Add the rest of the dressing and toss together gently. Taste and adjust the seasoning to your liking, then spoon onto the noodles and serve.

Serves 4

250 g buckwheat noodles

200 g soft tofu (not silken tofu)

100 g fresh shiitake mushrooms, finely sliced

3 spring onions, finely sliced

$\frac{1}{2}$ cup roughly chopped coriander leaves

3 tablespoons sesame seeds, toasted

3 tablespoons deep-fried shallots

salt

freshly ground black pepper

Dressing

3 tablespoons olive oil

3 drops of sesame oil

3 tablespoons rice-wine vinegar

3 tablespoons mirin

3 tablespoons low-sodium soy sauce

Vinegars

I think of vinegar as a kind of wonder-product! For a start there is something amazing about the fact it is produced by natural bacteria, and vinegar has many uses aside from cooking, such as cleaning and getting rid of smells around the kitchen.

Its culinary uses are not restricted to poaching eggs or whisking into salad dressings. I also like to splash vinegars into braised meat dishes where they add a hint of sweet sharpness, and they are great with fried foods, too. Think how a sprinkling of strong malt vinegar brings out the best in your fish-and-chip supper, or how spring rolls and dumplings cry out for a tangy, spicy dipping sauce. The vinegar cuts through the greasiness and livens up your palate.

In the following recipes I share my stepfather's technique for really maximising the flavour of the aromatics. It's brilliant. He briefly microwaves the vinegar and herbs. This speeds up the infusion process. But it's a good idea to microwave in short bursts, as the power of each oven varies.

CHILLI, GARLIC AND SOY VINEGAR

This is a tasty dipping sauce for spring rolls or Asian-style Pigeon (page 238), but also great to sprinkle on fried rice or noodle dishes for a bit of extra oomph.

2 garlic cloves	250 ml apple cider vinegar
2 small red chillies, split lengthwise and seeded	3 tablespoons soy sauce

Roughly smash the garlic cloves by putting them under the blade of a large knife turned on its side and pushing down on them, then peel away their skins. Combine with the remaining ingredients in a bottle. Place in a microwave and heat in 20-second bursts on full power for up to 60 seconds, or until the vinegar reaches 35–38°C on a thermometer. Cap with the lid and store in a cool, dark place. Leave for a week before using.

Makes 375 ml

TARRAGON VINEGAR

I asked my stepfather, a scientist and food-lover, for advice on making a srong-flavoured vinegar, and after a week mulling it over he came up with the freshest, most intensely tarragon-flavoured vinegar I'd ever tasted.

750 ml good-quality white wine vinegar, plus extra to top up the bottle

2 bunches tarragon

Combine the vinegar and tarragon in a wide-necked bottle. Place in a microwave and heat in 20-second bursts on full power for up to 60 seconds, or until the vinegar reaches 35–38°C on a thermometer. Cap with the lid and store in a cool, dark place for a week.

Strain the vinegar, discarding the tarragon, then pour back into a clean bottle. Top up with extra vinegar to fill the bottle if needed, then replace the lid and continue to store in a cool, dark place.

Makes 750 ml

GINGER AND CORIANDER VINEGAR

Use this as a dipping sauce for fried foods or dumplings, or in dressings for Asian-style salads and noodles. I also use it in marinades with soy and hoisin.

30 g ginger, peeled and finely sliced

½ cup roughly chopped coriander

375 ml apple cider vinegar, plus extra to top up the bottle

Combine the ingredients in a bottle. Place in a microwave and heat in 20-second bursts on full power for up to 60 seconds, or until the vinegar reaches 35–38°C on a thermometer. Cap with the lid and store in a cool, dark place for a week.

Strain the vinegar, discarding the ginger and coriander, then pour back into the cleaned-out bottle. Top up with extra vinegar to fill the bottle if needed, then replace the lid and continue to store in a cool, dark place.

Makes 375 ml

Oils

Many of us use oils almost on autopilot, grabbing at extra-virgin olive oil for salads, sesame oil for Asian noodles and vegetable oil for frying. Yes, they are a great cooking medium, but I often think oils deserve a bit more thought.

Oils help create wonderful crisp exteriors on the food we cook. They also help to bring the flavours of ingredients to life, and give a magical mouth-feel when we eat. I liberally splash all kinds of oil around in my kitchen and at the table. I brush a bit on a piece of grilled fish or steak before serving it up; drizzle it onto soups, casseroles and pastas; and of course toss it through salads.

Each oil has its own luscious flavour, whether it's pungent extra-virgin olive oil, fragrant nut oil, or unflavoured vegetable oil, useful for that very reason. Whichever oil you use, always make it the best quality you can afford. And make sure you store oils away from sunlight and heat.

PAPRIKA OIL

This pretty, pink-tinged oil adds a splash of colour and a warm, smoky flavour to salads. I also use it to baste meat as it barbecues, or drizzle it on just before serving.

2 fresh, blemish-free sprigs thyme

2 tablespoons smoked paprika

250 ml good-quality pure olive oil

Rub the thyme between the palms of your hands to release its essential oils. Put in a bottle with the remaining ingredients, cap with the lid and store in a cool, dark place for a week before using. (To speed up the infusion, you can gently warm the bottle in a saucepan of hot water or zap it without the lid for 20 seconds in a microwave.)

Once opened, continue to store in a cool, dark place, or refrigerate over the summer months.

Makes 250 ml

ROSEMARY AND GARLIC OIL

This is a really useful oil to have on hand for use in salad dressings and marinades, and for basting roast lamb or meat on the barbecue. I make the oil (and indeed all my flavoured oils) with a good-quality pure olive oil as extra-virgin olive oil has too strong a flavour.

4 garlic cloves
4 fresh, blemish-free rosemary sprigs

250 ml good-quality pure olive oil

Roughly smash the garlic cloves by putting them under the blade of a large knife turned on its side and pushing down on them. Peel away their skins and place in a jar. Cut the rosemary into lengths to fit the jar and rub between the palms of your hands to release its essential oils. Place in the jar, add the oil, cover with the lid and store in a cool, dark place for a week before using. (To speed up the infusion, you can gently warm the jar in a saucepan of hot water or zap it without the lid for 20 seconds in a microwave.) Once opened, continue to store in a cool, dark place.

Makes 250 ml

CHILLI AND GARLIC OIL

This is another brilliant oil for basting or marinating meat and poultry. I also use it in dressings and add the odd splash to soups and braises just before serving.

4 garlic cloves
3 small red chillies, split lengthwise and seeded

1 bay leaf
250 ml good-quality pure olive oil

Roughly smash the garlic cloves by putting them under the blade of a large knife turned on its side and pushing down on them. Peel away their skins and place in a bottle with the remaining ingredients. Cap with the lid and store in a cool, dark place for a week before using. (To speed up the infusion, you can gently warm the bottle in a saucepan of hot water or zap it without the lid for 20 seconds in a microwave.)

Once opened, continue to store in a cool, dark place, or refrigerate over the summer months.

Makes 250 ml

ARTICHOKE, MUSHROOM AND GARLIC DRESSING

To make the mushroom paste, whiz the mushrooms in a food processor until they are finely chopped.

Heat the oil in a large heavy-based frying pan. Add the onion and garlic and fry over medium heat for 5 minutes, or until soft and starting to colour. Add the mushrooms and thyme and fry for 10 minutes, or until the mushrooms are cooked and any liquid has evaporated. Season to taste, then remove from the heat and leave to cool. You should end up with about ½ cup of mushroom paste, known as duxelles.

Transfer the mushroom paste to a mixing bowl. Crush the garlic clove with the salt in a mortar and add to the mushrooms. Use a fork to mash the artichokes to a smoothish paste and add to the mushrooms, along with the remaining ingredients. Whisk everything together well, then taste and adjust the seasoning to your liking.

Store in a jar in a cool, dark place, or refrigerate over the summer months.

Makes 450 ml

Mushroom Paste

250 g swiss brown mushrooms, roughly chopped

3 tablespoons olive oil

½ small onion, finely diced

3 garlic cloves, crushed

1 tablespoon finely chopped thyme

salt

freshly ground black pepper

1 garlic clove

1 teaspoon salt

100 g artichoke hearts in oil, drained

3 tablespoons lemon juice

3 tablespoons white wine vinegar

80 ml extra-virgin olive oil

1 tablespoon chopped thyme

½ teaspoon freshly ground black pepper

SOUR CREAM AND CHIVE DRESSING

Spoon this into baked potatoes, mix through coleslaw or lettuce, or with anything you like. It's a classic combo that is simple and delicious.

250 ml sour cream

3 tablespoons extra-virgin olive oil

juice of 1 lemon

3 tablespoons finely snipped chives

½ teaspoon salt

½ teaspoon freshly ground white pepper

Whisk the ingredients together, then taste and adjust the seasoning to your liking. Refrigerate until ready to serve (it will keep for up to 7 days refrigerated).

Makes 380 ml

LEMON THYME AND MUSTARD DRESSING

Adding lemon thyme is quite a simple way of sprucing up a regular mustard dressing. It makes the best potato salad ever!

3 tablespoons dijon mustard

3 tablespoons French grain mustard

3 tablespoons brandy

juice of ½ lemon

80 ml extra-virgin olive oil

3 tablespoons finely chopped lemon thyme

1 teaspoon caster sugar

½ teaspoon freshly ground white pepper

Whisk all the ingredients together, then store in a jar in a cool, dark place. Refrigerate over the summer months.

Makes 210 ml

Seafood

Baked Snapper with Black Bean Butter

Pan-Fried Whiting with Salsa Verde

Sautéed Calamari

Kingfish Fillets with Malaysian Curry Spices

Tuna Niçoise

Michael's Spaghetti Marinara

Chilli Prawns

Mussels with White Wine and Rosemary

Scallops Baked on the Half-Shell
with Crunchy Herb Crumbs

Chilli Mud Crab

FISH has become a bit of a luxury item these days. It's expensive because it's a dwindling resource, and if we humans are not more careful about the way we manage the world's fish supplies, the day will inevitably come when it's just not there for us to eat anymore.

What is also so unfortunate about the whole over-fishing problem is that seafood is so good for us. From a health perspective alone, we should actually be eating more food from the sea. It's especially true of the oily fish like mackerel, salmon, sardines and tuna, which are chock-full of omega-3 fatty acids. (These are great for heart health, and research also suggests that they can protect against strokes and some cancers and improve arthritis symptoms.)

But we need to treat fish with as much respect as we have started to do with meat and poultry. We need to think about making sustainable choices (and there's loads of information around on the internet and even from your local fish shop). The beauty of adopting this approach is that many of the less-threatened species are a bit less expensive — but they are no less delicious.

When it comes to cooking fish, less is more. Most fish and seafood has a delicate texture and flavour, so the last thing you want to do is mess around with it too much. Often all you need to do is pan-fry it in a bit of butter with a sprinkling of fresh herbs or a drizzle of flavoured oil. When I add a sauce, it will inevitably be a simple, fresh-tasting one that brings out the flavour of the fish itself.

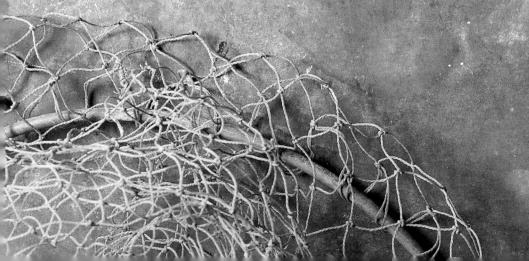

BAKED SNAPPER WITH BLACK BEAN BUTTER

As with meat and poultry, fish tastes so much sweeter when it's cooked whole. Baking it *'en papilotte'* — in a paper or foil parcel — is the best way to do this as it seals in all the juices and flavour and keeps the fish lovely and moist. The added benefit is that the bag puffs up dramatically in the oven and looks really impressive when you take it to the table. This method does work best in an oven, although you can do it in a barbecue with a hood. Just remember not to have any heat directly beneath the fish parcel.

Whole snapper are ideal baking fish. In this recipe the fish is married with Asian flavours — ginger and fermented black beans, whose strong saltiness is mellowed out beautifully by the butter, herbs and natural juices. It's one of my all-time-favourite dishes (and it also works for snapper fillets if that's what you'd prefer).

Preheat the oven to 200°C and lightly oil a large baking tray.

Use a sharp knife to make deep slashes on either side of the fish and season the cuts generously with salt and pepper.

Cut a sheet of baking paper large enough to wrap around the fish and lay it out on your work surface. Smear a little of the butter onto the paper, then scatter on the snow-pea shoots. Sit the fish on top and cover with the remaining ingredients and the rest of the butter. Wrap the paper around the fish and fold in the ends to seal. Now wrap this package in a double layer of foil and lift onto the prepared tray.

Bake for 10–15 minutes, by which time the fish should be cooked and the bag should be all puffed up (a very thick fish may take a few minutes more). Open the parcel at the table to release the lovely aromas. Serve with lime wedges.

Serves 2

900 g snapper, cleaned and scaled

salt

freshly ground black pepper

100 g butter, cubed

200 g snow-pea shoots

3 spring onions, sliced

1 tablespoon finely sliced ginger

3 tablespoons roughly chopped coriander (stalks and leaves)

1 teaspoon fermented black beans, roughly chopped

a few thin slices of small red chilli (optional)

a few drops of sesame oil (or $\frac{1}{4}$ teaspoon toasted sesame seeds)

lime wedges to serve

PAN-FRIED WHITING WITH SALSA VERDE

King George whiting is a delicate white-fleshed fish that lives in shallow waters near the coastline. Because the fillets are small and thin, they need to be treated gently. They can be cooked skin-side up on an oiled oven tray under an overhead grill, or pan-fried, as they are here.

Pat the whiting fillets dry with paper towel, then season them generously all over with salt and pepper. Heat the oil in a large heavy-based frying pan over medium heat. When it starts to sizzle, add the fillets skin-side down and fry for a minute or so. Turn them carefully, then add the butter and parsley to the pan. Cook for another 30 seconds, then lift carefully onto serving plates. Pour a little of the parsley butter over each serve and accompany with salsa verde and lemon wedges.

Serves 4

8 whiting fillets, skin on

salt

freshly ground black pepper

3 tablespoons olive oil

2 tablespoons butter

2 tablespoons finely chopped flat-leaf parsley

125 ml Salsa Verde (page 27)

lemon wedges to serve

SAUTÉED CALAMARI

I like to use southern calamari as it's widely available. I use the bodies, tentacles, wings — in fact, everything except the innards!

To prepare the calamari, cut the bodies and wings into 1 cm slices. Cut the tentacles into individual legs.

Combine the oil, garlic and chilli in a large heavy-based frying pan. Heat gently until the garlic and chilli start to fry and the kitchen fills with delicious aromas. As soon as the garlic starts to colour, add the calamari. Increase the heat to medium–high and cook until the calamari begins to turn milky-white, then season with salt and pepper and add the spinach. Leave for a minute, then as the spinach starts to wilt, turn everything over in the pan and cook for another 20 seconds or so.

Serve hot from the pan with lemon wedges.

Serves 4 as a starter

2 medium calamari, cleaned (to yield around 400 g)

2 tablespoons olive oil

1 garlic clove, finely chopped

1 small red chilli, finely sliced (seeds removed if you don't like too much heat)

salt

freshly ground black pepper

250 g baby spinach leaves

lemon wedges to serve

KINGFISH FILLETS WITH MALAYSIAN CURRY SPICES

When I was a boy, my family lived in Malaysia for several years, and this dish takes me right back to the island of Penang. Kingfish is ideal for this sort of curry, as its flesh is slightly oily and firm and it absorbs other flavours well.

Heat the oil in a large heavy-based saucepan. Add the onion and fry over medium heat for 5 minutes, or until soft and starting to colour. Add the garlic, lemongrass, chilli, ginger and turmeric and fry gently for 2–3 minutes. Stir in the palm sugar followed by the tomato passata, coconut milk and strained tamarind water. Bring to a boil, then lower the heat and simmer for 20 minutes, stirring from time to time.

Add the kingfish fillets and return to a simmer. Cook for 10–15 minutes, or until the fish is just cooked through.

When ready to serve, stir in the lime juice and coriander. Garnish with the peanuts and coconut and serve with coconut rice.

Serves 4

3 tablespoons vegetable oil

1 onion, finely sliced

4 garlic cloves, crushed

1 lemongrass stalk, bruised with the back of a knife and cut in half

1 small red chilli, sliced

1 tablespoon grated ginger

1 tablespoon grated fresh turmeric (or ground turmeric if unavailable)

2 tablespoons grated palm sugar

250 ml Tomato Passata (for recipe see page 156)

750 ml coconut milk

2 tablespoons tamarind pulp softened in 250 ml warm water

800 g kingfish fillets

juice of 1 lime

1 cup chopped coriander leaves

2 tablespoons peanuts, roasted and chopped

2 tablespoons desiccated coconut, lightly toasted

TUNA NIÇOISE

Niçoise salad is usually made with tinned tuna, which is fine for a quick and easy meal. But when you want to be a bit more fancy, it's lovely to use fresh tuna. You can grill or sear it to make a warm salad, of course, but my favourite way of all is to steep it overnight in a light, herby brine. It ends up really moist and flavoursome — a bit like a posh version of the tinned stuff, only so much better!

When shopping for tuna, look for yellowfin — it's the best option now that bluefin stocks have been almost fished out.

To brine the tuna, set a wire rack inside a small, deep tray that is just large enough to accommodate the tuna steaks. Combine the water, vinegar, salt, sugar, chillies and rosemary in a large saucepan and bring to a boil, then remove from the heat. Pour a third of the hot brine into the tray. Sit the tuna steaks on the rack and pour the remaining brine over the top. The tuna should be completely submerged. Leave to cool, then cover and refrigerate overnight.

Whisk the dressing ingredients together and set aside until ready to use.

Combine the salad ingredients except the eggs in a large mixing bowl. Pour on the dressing and toss together gently. Divide between 4 bowls. Remove the tuna steaks from the brine and crumble them roughly into each salad. Peel the eggs and cut them in half, and add them to the top of each salad. Serve with crusty bread.

Serves 4

Tuna

800 ml water

200 ml Tarragon Vinegar (page 43)

50 g salt

20 g sugar

2 small red chillies

2 rosemary sprigs

4 x 150 g tuna steaks

Salad

200 g green beans, trimmed and blanched

200 g kipfler potatoes, peeled, boiled and sliced into 1 cm rounds

2 red capsicums, seeded and finely sliced

3 spring onions, sliced

40 g black or green olives, pitted

$\frac{1}{4}$ cup roughly chopped flat-leaf parsley

$\frac{1}{4}$ cup basil leaves

4 anchovy fillets, sliced lengthwise

4 eggs, soft-boiled

Dressing

3 tablespoons extra-virgin olive oil

juice of 1 lemon

2 tablespoons Tarragon Vinegar (page 43)

2 tablespoons French grain mustard

salt

freshly ground black pepper

MICHAEL'S SPAGHETTI MARINARA

I was taught how to make this classic dish by expert seafood chef Michael Bacash, who runs a well-known Melbourne restaurant. In the two years I worked for Michael, I learnt a huge amount about how to select, prepare and cook all kinds of fish and seafood, and I now share this knowledge with the young chefs in my own restaurant.

When it comes to seafood, one of the most important things is to buy the best quality and the freshest available.

Bring a large saucepan of salted water to a boil and add the pasta, cooking until al dente (it usually takes 8–10 minutes).

Meanwhile, heat the oil in a large frying pan or wok. Add the garlic and chilli and cook over medium heat until the garlic starts to colour. Add the seafood to the pan and increase the heat to high. Cook, turning the seafood continuously. By the time the mussels open, all the seafood should be cooked, and the pasta should be ready or almost.

When the pasta is cooked, drain it and add to the pan with the seafood. Stir in the parsley and season with salt and pepper. Toss gently to combine.

Serve straight away, dividing evenly between 4 shallow bowls.

Serves 4

200 g dried spaghetti or linguine

3 tablespoons olive oil

4 garlic cloves, chopped

1 teaspoon finely sliced small red chilli (or more or less to taste)

8 large prawns, shelled and deveined

100 g calamari rings

500 g mussels, scrubbed and de-bearded

100 g scallops, intestinal tracts removed

100 g white fish, bones removed and cut into 2 cm dice

$\frac{1}{2}$ cup chopped flat-leaf parsley

salt

freshly ground black pepper

CHILLI PRAWNS

There are those who say that if you use too much chilli you can't taste the other ingredients. I say, don't listen to them! But if you really are averse to too much heat, then make adjustments in this recipe to suit, such as discard the seeds, use fewer chillies, or use milder flavoured long red chillies.

This is a really speedy dish, and a good one for spring evenings when the days are getting longer and you can dine in the back garden with a few cold beers. Prawns cook in no time at all, so take them off the heat as soon as they begin to turn opaque. That way they'll stay moist and juicy and will have a lovely texture.

Heat the oil in a large heavy-based frying pan. Add the onion and cook over medium heat for 3–4 minutes, or until it begins to soften and colour. Add the garlic, chilli, anchovy (if using) and paprika and cook for a minute.

Increase the heat to high, add the prawns and season with salt and pepper. Cook the prawns for 2–3 minutes, turning halfway through. Add the herbs and lemon juice, toss quickly and serve straight away with warm crusty bread.

Serves 4

125 ml olive oil

1 large red onion, finely sliced

6 garlic cloves, roughly chopped

2 small red chillies, finely sliced

1 anchovy fillet (optional)

1 tablespoon smoked paprika

20 raw king prawns, shelled and deveined, heads left on

salt

freshly ground black pepper

1 cup roughly chopped flat-leaf parsley

$\frac{1}{2}$ cup roughly chopped coriander leaves

juice of $\frac{1}{2}$ lemon

MUSSELS WITH WHITE WINE AND ROSEMARY

This is my version of a classic and ever-popular way of preparing mussels. Make sure you use a pan with a tight-fitting lid to ensure the mussels steam open successfully. And buy the freshest mussels you can from a reputable fishmonger; that way you will really taste the sea. This is a roll-up-your-sleeves kind of dish, to be eaten with your fingers and plenty of crusty bread to mop up the juices.

Heat the oil in a large heavy-based saucepan over high heat. Add the garlic, chilli, tomato, mussels and herbs, then pour in the wine. Cover the pan with a lid and shake a few times. Cook for 5–6 minutes, shaking occasionally.

Remove the lid and check to see whether the mussels have all opened — some may not have. Shake the pan vigorously and cook, covered, for another minute, then discard any mussels that still refuse to open. Season to taste (remembering that the mussels are already quite salty), then tip into a large serving bowl. Drizzle on the ouzo, scatter on the parsley and serve straight away with plenty of crusty bread.

Serves 4 as a starter

$2\frac{1}{2}$ tablespoons extra-virgin olive oil

1 garlic clove, crushed

1 small red chilli, finely chopped (remove the seeds if you don't like too much heat)

3 roma tomatoes, diced

1 kg mussels, scrubbed and de-bearded

handful of basil leaves

rosemary sprig

100 ml white wine

salt

freshly ground black pepper

$1\frac{1}{2}$ tablespoons ouzo

$\frac{1}{2}$ cup finely chopped flat-leaf parsley

SCALLOPS BAKED ON THE HALF-SHELL WITH CRUNCHY HERB CRUMBS

When I was a teenager, one of my biggest treats was to go scuba diving in Port Phillip Bay with my father. He taught me how to swim along the ocean floor looking for scallops, and how to catch them in a small sack. We'd always go home with a good catch, and in my memory they were so sweet and buttery that they barely needed any cooking at all.

These days scallops are readily available, although it can be harder to find them on the half-shell. Resist the temptation to rinse them as it washes all their natural juices away. To clean them, you just need to remove the dark intestinal tracts and pull off any bits of beard, but make sure you leave the lovely orange coral attached. Give the shell a bit of a wipe if you see any obvious bits of sand or grit, but try not to detach the scallop.

Preheat the oven to 200°C.

Put the butter and garlic in a mixing bowl and beat with electric beaters until pale and fluffy. Briefly beat in the salt and pepper, then fold in the herbs and breadcrumbs.

Sit the scallops on a large tray and divide the butter mixture evenly between them — there should be around 2 tablespoons per scallop. Bake in the oven for 5–10 minutes, or until the butter is bubbling and the crumbs are golden brown. Serve straight away with lemon wedges and fresh bread to mop up the herby juices.

Serves 4 as a starter

150 g butter at room temperature

3 garlic cloves, crushed

pinch of salt

pinch of freshly ground black pepper

3 tablespoons chopped flat-leaf parsley

2 tablespoons chopped thyme

2 tablespoons chopped dill

$\frac{1}{2}$ cup dried sourdough breadcrumbs

12 scallops on the half-shell, intestinal tracts removed, and any bits of beard, sand or shell wiped off

lemon wedges to serve

CHILLI MUD CRAB

This is a fantastic dish from Singapore that everyone seems to love. It ain't pretty to eat, but I guarantee people will be licking their fingers.

Ideally, buy your mud crab live and put it in the freezer for a few hours to put it to sleep and thus kill it humanely.

Remove the top shell from the crab and discard the brown 'mustard', the feathery gills (dead man's fingers) and the bony bits at the head. Remove the front claws and bash them with a rolling pin to crack the shell. Use a heavy knife to cut the crab in half, then cut between each leg to give you 6 pieces to add to the 2 claws.

Heat the oil in a large wok over medium heat. Add the shallots and fry until golden. Add the garlic, chilli and ginger and stir-fry for 1–2 minutes. Add the sauces, vinegar, water and sugar and bring to a simmer.

Add the crab pieces to the wok and spoon the hot sauce over them. Simmer for 8–10 minutes, by which time the shells should have turned bright red and the meat will be cooked. Stir in the cornflour to thicken the sauce. Scatter on the coriander and spring onions and serve immediately with lots of napkins and finger bowls.

Serves 4

1 mud crab weighing approximately 1 kg

3 tablespoons vegetable oil

4 shallots, finely sliced

3 garlic cloves, crushed

3 small red chillies, finely sliced

1 tablespoon grated ginger

250 ml tomato sauce

3 tablespoons kecap manis (Indonesian sweet soy sauce)

3 tablespoons soy sauce

2 tablespoons hoisin sauce

1 tablespoon fish sauce

2 tablespoons rice wine vinegar

125 ml water

3 tablespoons sugar

3 tablespoons cornflour mixed with 1 tablespoon water

1 cup roughly chopped coriander leaves

4 spring onions, finely sliced

Masterclass

HOW TO MAKE LABNE

1 kg thick natural yoghurt

1 teaspoon salt

extra-virgin olive oil to drizzle
if making soft labne

good-quality pure olive oil to cover
if making firm labne balls

1 cup finely chopped herbs such as
flat-leaf parsley, chives, coriander,
mint or dill (one or a combination)
to coat balls if desired

VARIATIONS

✻ 1 garlic clove crushed
   with 1 teaspoon salt

or

✻ 1 tablespoon dijon mustard

or

✻ 1 tablespoon harissa paste

SERVING SUGGESTIONS

*Labne is great as an antipasto; with
kebabs or kofte; smeared on burger
buns; or as a base for dips.*

1 Combine the yoghurt and salt in a mixing bowl and stir together
thoroughly. If making one of the variations, stir the ingredient
into the yoghurt now.

2 Line a colander or large sieve with 2 large squares of muslin
(a clean tea towel will also do the job). Spoon in the yoghurt.

3 Bring in the corners of the muslin and tie together tightly, or tie
up with string.

4 Suspend the bundle from a wooden spoon set over a bowl and
refrigerate for up to 3 or 4 days. The longer you hang the labne,
the firmer it will be. After 1 day it will be a very thick and creamy
cheese spread.

5 To serve the labne after 1 day, unwrap it and tip into a serving
bowl. Drizzle with extra-virgin olive oil and serve with Arabic
or crusty bread, or as a dip with crudités.

6 If you continue draining the yoghurt for 3 or 4 days, you will be
able to form it into balls, which you may leave plain or roll in
herbs. Lightly oil your hands and roll the labne into balls the size
of large marbles. Roll in herbs if desired. Place in a large jar and
cover with olive oil. The balls will keep in the refrigerator for up
to 2 weeks.

Makes 600 g soft labne (after 1 day) or 400 g firm labne
(after 3–4 days)

Barbecues

THE PERFECT STEAK

PRAWNS WRAPPED IN PANCETTA

STICKY, SMOKY PORK RIBS

SWEET 'N' STICKY 'CHICKETY' WINGS

SWEET CHICKEN SKEWERS WRAPPED IN PROSCIUTTO

TURKISH-SPICED KOFTE KEBABS

GRILLED EGGPLANT WITH GREEN OLIVE
AND HERB SALSA

BARBECUED HALOUMI WRAPPED IN ZUCCHINI

MAN, FOOD, FLAMES: the barbecue is one of the oldest and best ways of cooking. And I say 'man', because if there's one area of cooking that men really do relish, it's the barbie. I reckon it must be something deep inside us that yearns to get back to those primitive, primeval days!

In the twenty-first century we're a bit more sophisticated, and you can spend your money on all sorts of fancy barbecues with various bells and whistles. The gas-fired sorts do have the advantage of speed, but honestly, given a choice, I'll go for a solid-fuel flame every time. Good barbecuing over real fire just makes your food smell and taste irresistible. Plus you have the option of adding an extra smoky perfume by using different woods and coals or branches of fresh, woody herbs like thyme, rosemary or bay leaves.

Here are a few hints to help you get the best out of your barbecue. First of all, don't try to cook over the flames themselves or you'll end up with burnt, blackened food! If you're cooking over charcoal or wood, then wait for the fire to die down to glowing embers, or if you are using a gas barbie, then position your food to the side of the flames so it is not sitting directly on top. The second hint is that you can move your food around from high heat to medium heat when you need to, and don't have to let it just sit there — you've got great control with barbecue cooking, so use your power! Third, be careful with oily marinades or fatty meat that can drip and cause flare-ups. Flare-ups lead to charring, which will spoil the flavour of your food.

In addition to some great barbecue dishes, I'm including recipes for some of my favourite 'flavour enhancers'. These are the marinades, pastes and spice rubs that I use to bring barbecues to life.

Marinades

GREEK HERB MARINADE

Use this herby marinade for all cuts of lamb. It's also good for brushing onto vegetables on the barbecue, and I use it for Barbecued Haloumi Wrapped in Zucchini (page 94).

Whisk the ingredients together in a mixing bowl. If not using immediately, transfer to a jar and store in the refrigerator, where it will keep for up to 1 month.

When ready to use, pour the marinade over your meat, turning the meat to coat evenly, then cover and refrigerate for at least 1 hour or up to overnight to allow the flavours to develop.

Makes 250 ml

2 tablespoons chopped thyme

1 tablespoon chopped sage leaves

2 tablespoons dried oregano

1 tablespoon freshly ground black pepper

1 tablespoon fennel seeds, ground

1 garlic clove, crushed

grated zest of $\frac{1}{2}$ lemon and juice of whole lemon

180 ml olive oil

SPICY DRY RUB FOR BEEF STEAK

I'm a big fan of spice rubs, which, along with marinades, are a great way of livening up the flavour of your barbecue meats and poultry.

This rub will be sufficient to coat around 1 kilogram of steak. Any unused mixture can be stored in an airtight container.

Mix all the ingredients together. If not using immediately, store in an airtight container and use within 1 month.

When ready to use, massage the mixture into your steak, coating well. Cover and refrigerate for at least 1 hour or up to overnight to allow the flavours to develop.

Makes 55 g

2 tablespoons ground coriander, toasted

2 tablespoons smoked paprika

1 tablespoon dried oregano

1 tablespoon dried chilli flakes

1 teaspoon cayenne pepper

1 tablespoon salt

1 teaspoon freshly ground black pepper

1 teaspoon freshly ground white pepper

STICKY RIB MARINADE, MEXICAN-STYLE

Dried Mexican chillies add a unique smoky flavour to this marinade. You'll find them in specialist Spanish or South American food stores, and they are also available online from mail-order suppliers. This marinade is brilliant with pork or beef ribs, or even chicken wings. The quantities here will be sufficient for 2–3 kilograms of meat, but any leftover marinade can be stored in the refrigerator for up to two months.

Place the ingredients in a food processor and whiz to a paste. If not using immediately, transfer to a jar and store in the refrigerator, where it will keep for up to 2 months.

When ready to use, pour the marinade over the ribs, turning them to coat evenly, then cover and refrigerate for at least 1 hour or up to overnight to allow the flavours to develop.

Makes 400 ml

30 g dried mulato or chipotle chillies

30 g dried ancho chillies

2 garlic cloves

½ cup roughly chopped coriander leaves

1 tablespoon smoked paprika

1 tablespoon cayenne pepper

1 teaspoon ground star anise

100 g brown sugar

1 ½ tablespoons salt

1 tablespoon freshly ground black pepper

250 ml apple cider vinegar

3 tablespoons olive oil

KICK-ASS CHILLI MARINADE

Marinades are all about adding flavour, and this one adds it in spades! And it's not really all about the chilli, even though I do like things blisteringly hot. You can vary the heat, depending on the amount and type of chillies you use: some varieties (such as small red bullet chillies or habaneros) are good for ramping up the heat; others (such as long red chillies, jalapeños or dried ancho, chipotle or mulato chillies) add milder spice and unique flavours.

I like to experiment with a combination of fresh and dried chillies, so you should feel free to do the same.

Combine the ingredients except the coriander and lemon juice in a bowl and mix well. If not using immediately, transfer to a jar and store in the refrigerator, where it will keep for up to 1 month.

When ready to use, add the coriander and lemon juice. Pour the marinade over your meat, turning it to coat evenly, then cover and refrigerate for at least 1 hour or up to overnight to allow the flavours to develop.

Makes 500 ml

3 tablespoons ground cumin, toasted

3 tablespoons ground coriander, toasted

3 tablespoons freshly ground black pepper

2 tablespoons cayenne pepper

1 tablespoon fennel seeds, ground

3 tablespoons dried chilli flakes

3 tablespoons finely chopped small red chillies

1 teaspoon salt

275 ml vegetable oil

$\frac{1}{2}$ cup chopped coriander leaves

squeeze of lemon juice

THE PERFECT STEAK

People can agonise over cooking steak — which is a shame because there's nothing to beat the flavour of a lovely, juicy piece of top-notch beef. And it's got to be one of the simplest meals around, as all it needs is a bit of salad and a dollop of your favourite mustard or relish. For extra flavour, brush the steaks with a sprig of rosemary during cooking, and squeeze over some lemon before serving.

4 x 350 g porterhouse steaks (or for something special, rib-eye steaks on the bone)

extra-virgin olive oil

salt flakes

freshly ground black pepper

sprig of rosemary and a lemon (optional)

Remove the steaks from the refrigerator at least 30 minutes before you want to eat. Preheat your barbecue grill to medium–high.

Rub the steaks all over with a little oil and season generously with salt and pepper.

Put the steaks on the grill and cook for 2 minutes, then turn over and cook for a further 2 minutes. Turn over again, this time placing the steaks on a 90-degree angle, and cook for another 2 minutes. Turn over for a final time, keeping the steaks on the angle, and cook for another 2 minutes. By this time the steaks should be cooked medium–rare and should be neatly crosshatched with marks from the grill.

Testing a steak for doneness is probably the thing that people worry about most. One sure way to remove all the guesswork is to invest in a meat thermometer — you won't regret it. Check the interior of the meat with the probe: 35°C = rare; 45°C = medium–rare; 55°C = medium; 65°C = medium–well; 75°C = well done. If you don't have a thermometer, you can press the steak with your finger — essentially, the more yielding the steak is under pressure, the rarer the steak is. A guideline is the thumb-to-finger test. Feel the fleshy base between your thumb and index finger as you touch your thumb to each of your fingers: thumb to index finger = rare; thumb to middle finger = medium–rare; thumb to ring finger = medium to medium–well; thumb to little finger = well done. Remember that it is better to undercook than to overcook!

Before serving your steaks, transfer them to a warm plate, cover loosely with foil and leave to rest for at least 4 minutes before serving. This is the most important step of all, as it allows the juices to settle back into the centre of the meat, and for all the fibres to relax, becoming nice and tender. If you cut straight into your steak without letting it rest, all the juices will rush out and it will be dry.

Serves 4

PRAWNS WRAPPED IN PANCETTA

I like to think of these as 'prawns kilpatrick'! The sweet and salty flavour of pancetta — an Italian bacon, a kind of poor cousin to prosciutto — is wonderful with the prawns, and it also helps to protect the delicate prawn meat from the heat of the barbecue. Prawns with their heads still on make for a great presentation.

Combine the oil, lemon zest and pepper in a small bowl, forming a runny paste. Brush onto the prawns, then wrap the body of each prawn with a sage leaf and a slice of pancetta. Thread onto long metal skewers (keeping the natural curve of the prawns), aiming for 6 per skewer, or as many as possible without overcrowding.

Preheat your barbecue grill to medium. While it is heating, gently mix the salsa ingredients together.

Grill the prawns for a few minutes on each side, or until the pancetta is crisp and brown and the prawns are cooked through. Serve immediately with the salsa.

Serves 4

3 tablespoons olive oil

grated zest of 1 lemon

freshly ground black pepper

24 king prawns, shelled and deveined, heads left on

24 sage leaves

24 thin slices of pancetta

Tomato and Chive Salsa

4 roma tomatoes, cut into 1 cm dice

3 tablespoons finely snipped chives

1 tablespoon chopped flat-leaf parsley

2 tablespoons sherry vinegar

3 tablespoons extra-virgin olive oil

salt

freshly ground black pepper

STICKY, SMOKY PORK RIBS

Adding woodchips to the coals in your barbecue is a great way of infusing an irresistible smoky flavour to your meal — but they work best with a kettle barbecue (one with a hood). You can find hickory woodchips at most DIY stores, or wherever barbecues are sold. Pork-belly spare ribs need long, slow cooking, which really gives time for the smoky flavours to penetrate the meat. Serve with Dirty Mojitos (page 139) and lots of napkins to wipe those sticky fingers.

Combine the sticky rub ingredients in a large mixing bowl. Use your hands to rub the mixture into the spare ribs. Cover with plastic wrap and leave to marinate in the refrigerator overnight, or for up to 2 days. Turn the meat around in the marinade every 6 hours or so.

When ready to cook, light a fire in your kettle barbecue. When the coals die down to about 160°C, scatter a small handful of hickory woodchips onto the coals to create smoke. Sit the ribs on the grill, pull down the hood on the barbecue and cook the ribs for 3 hours. Every 45 minutes or so, add a few more woodchips to keep the smoke going.

When the ribs are cooked, they should be wonderfully soft and tender, enough to fall apart in your hands. Serve with lemon wedges.

Serves 4

2 kg pork-belly spare ribs
lemon wedges to serve

Sticky Rub
4 tablespoons brown sugar
1 tablespoon caraway seeds, ground
1 tablespoon ground ginger
1 tablespoon dried chilli flakes
2 tablespoons chopped coriander leaves
1 tablespoon freshly ground black pepper
1 teaspoon salt

SWEET 'N' STICKY 'CHICKETY' WINGS

Chicken wings are almost always the first thing I throw on the barbie when I'm entertaining. I love them, my friends love them, and most importantly of all, so do all the kids!

Chicken wings need to be cooked until they're sticky with lots of crunchy crisp bits. And here's a bit of barbecue etiquette: make sure there's a bucket close to hand for all the bones; stock up on paper napkins; and have a few finger bowls dotted around the place — they sound posh, but they are just bowls of warm water with a bit of lemon juice squeezed in.

This is a kid-friendly recipe, but feel free to crank up the heat and add 1–2 tablespoons of dried chilli flakes to the marinade if you're cooking for adults.

Mix the marinade ingredients in a large mixing bowl.

Use a sharp knife to cut a few incisions in each chicken wing, then add them to the marinade and toss until evenly coated. Cover and refrigerate for at least 1 hour, or preferably overnight, to allow the flavours to develop.

Remove the chicken wings from the refrigerator at least 30 minutes before you want to eat. Preheat your barbecue grill to medium–high.

Put the chicken wings on the grill and cook for about 20 minutes, turning them frequently to make sure they don't burn. At the end of the cooking time they should be a lovely, sticky golden brown. Pile them onto a large platter and scatter on the parsley. Serve straight away with lemon wedges and lots of napkins.

Serves 6

2 kg free-range chicken wings

½ cup roughly chopped flat-leaf parsley

lemon wedges to serve

Marinade

3 tablespoons kecap manis (Indonesian sweet soy sauce)

3 garlic cloves, crushed

½ cup chopped coriander leaves

2 tablespoons grated ginger

2 tablespoons dried oregano

2 tablespoons brown sugar

1 teaspoon freshly ground black pepper

zest and juice of 2 lemons

3 tablespoons sherry vinegar

3 tablespoons olive oil

SWEET CHICKEN SKEWERS WRAPPED IN PROSCIUTTO

These chicken skewers are a cut above your average, as the prosciutto wrapping becomes lovely and crunchy on the barbecue and adds a great salty flavour to complement the sweet marinade. It's a good idea to cook them over low–medium heat or the prosciutto will char too quickly.

Mix the marinade ingredients in a large mixing bowl. Add the chicken pieces and toss until evenly coated. Cover and refrigerate overnight to allow the flavours to develop.

Remove the chicken from the refrigerator at least 30 minutes before you want to eat. Preheat your barbecue grill to low–medium.

Remove the chicken pieces from the marinade and season lightly with salt. Wrap each piece of chicken in a slice of prosciutto and thread onto 4 long metal skewers, allowing 7 pieces on each. Brush lightly with oil and cook for 10–15 minutes, turning frequently to make sure the prosciutto doesn't burn. Arrange on a platter and serve straight away.

Serves 4

4 free-range chicken breasts, cut into 28 pieces

salt

28 thin slices of prosciutto

olive oil

Marinade

2 tablespoons brown sugar

1 tablespoon smoked paprika

1 teaspoon freshly ground white pepper

2 garlic cloves, crushed

2 tablespoons grated ginger

$\frac{1}{2}$ cup chopped flat-leaf parsley

zest and juice of 1 lemon

2 tablespoons apple cider vinegar

2 tablespoons sweet sherry

3 tablespoons olive oil

TURKISH-SPICED KOFTE KEBABS

'Kofte' means minced meat — either as meatballs or moulded around long, flat skewers to make kebabs. You'll find them all around the Middle East and eastern Mediterranean, but this particular recipe is Turkish. Stuff them into pockets of warm pita bread with salad and serve with a tasty dressing. Sour Cream and Chive Dressing (page 47), Minted Yoghurt (page 120) or Indian Spiced Tomato Chutney (page 176) would all be brilliant.

Combine all the ingredients in a large mixing bowl. Use your hands to squish everything together thoroughly, until the onion, garlic, spices and herbs are evenly distributed. Cover and refrigerate for 20 minutes to allow the flavours to develop.

When ready to cook, preheat a barbecue grill to high. Use wet hands to divide the kofte mixture into 12 portions and mould each around a flat metal skewer into a long sausage shape. (It's important to use flat skewers as the meat won't stick to long skinny ones.)

Cook the kofte for 5–8 minutes, turning frequently, until they are golden brown and cooked through. Serve with pita bread, salad and yoghurt or your choice of dressing.

Serves 4–6

1 kg minced lamb leg or shoulder

$\frac{1}{2}$ onion, finely diced

2 garlic cloves, crushed

1 tablespoon cumin seeds, toasted and ground

1 teaspoon coriander seeds, toasted and ground

1 teaspoon chilli powder

1 teaspoon fennel seeds, ground

1 teaspoon ground allspice

1 teaspoon ground ginger

1 tablespoon salt

1 tablespoon freshly ground black pepper

3 tablespoons chopped coriander leaves

$\frac{1}{2}$ cup chopped flat-leaf parsley

grated zest of $\frac{1}{2}$ lemon

GRILLED EGGPLANT WITH GREEN OLIVE AND HERB SALSA

This very simple vegetable dish is bursting with flavour. It could serve as part of a barbecue spread or as a main dish for vegetarians. If you run out of time to salt the eggplants, it's probably not the end of the world, but I do think it improves their flavour.

Layer the eggplant slices in a tray, scattering generously with salt as you go. Cover with plastic wrap, weight with a chopping board and leave for 1 hour.

To make the salsa, combine the ingredients in a bowl and mix together thoroughly. You can make this salsa in advance and store in the refrigerator.

Preheat a barbecue grill to medium–high. Rinse the eggplant in cold water and pat dry with paper towel. Place in a large mixing bowl and season with an a little salt and pepper. Add the olive oil and toss until the slices are evenly coated.

Cook the eggplant slices for 2–3 minutes on each side, until golden brown. Transfer to a serving platter and spoon on the salsa.

Serves 4

2 large eggplants, cut into 2 cm slices

salt

1 tablespoon freshly ground black pepper

80 ml olive oil

Salsa

3 tablespoons roughly chopped flat-leaf parsley

3 tablespoons roughly chopped basil leaves

3 tablespoons snipped chives

3 tablespoons roughly chopped dill

80 ml extra-virgin olive oil

200 g green olives, pitted and roughly chopped

2 tablespoons Tarragon Vinegar (page 43)

juice of 2 lemons

salt

freshly ground black pepper

BARBECUED HALOUMI WRAPPED IN ZUCCHINI

Vegetarians often feel badly done-by when it comes to barbecues, as the focus tends to be firmly on meat, poultry or seafood. These haloumi skewers make a really tasty vegetarian option — and they look so attractive that meat-eaters might even be jealous!

Haloumi is a firm white cheese that stands up well to the heat of the barbecue. The trick is to slice the zucchini wafer-thin. Use the slicing groove on your cheese grater or, even better, a mandolin — but watch your fingers!

Toss the cubes of haloumi in the marinade and cover and refrigerate for at least 20 minutes, up to overnight, to allow the flavours to develop.

To make the capsicum dressing, combine the ingredients in a food processor and blend to a smooth sauce. Refrigerate until ready to use.

When ready to cook, preheat a barbecue grill to medium–high. Wrap a slice of zucchini around each cube of haloumi, then thread onto skewers. Cook for 2–3 minutes on each side, until the zucchini is coloured and the cheese is softening. Serve straight away with the capsicum dressing.

Serves 4

600 g haloumi, cut into 4 cm cubes

125 ml Greek Herb Marinade (page 76)

2 large zucchini, ends trimmed and sliced wafer-thin

Capsicum Dressing

1 large red capsicum, roasted, peeled, seeded and roughly chopped

2 ripe roma tomatoes, roughly chopped

3 tablespoons roughly chopped coriander leaves

$\frac{1}{2}$ garlic clove, crushed

3 tablespoons extra-virgin olive oil

3 tablespoons lemon juice

salt

freshly ground black pepper

Bread

GREEN OLIVE ROLLS

POTATO BREAD

PIZZA DOUGH

Masterclass

HOW TO MAKE FOCACCIA

1¼ teaspoons dried yeast

1½ tablespoons warm water

500 g plain flour

½ tablespoon salt

280 ml water at room temperature

olive oil

1 tablespoon smoked paprika (preferably Spanish)

½ tablespoon chopped rosemary, plus extra leaves or small sprigs

salt flakes

NOTE

Other ingredients that work well sprinkled on focaccia are olives, ground cumin or slices of garlic.

1 Whisk the yeast and warm water in a small bowl and leave for about 10 minutes to activate.

2 Put the flour and salt in a large mixing bowl. Add the room-temperature water and 1 tablespoon of olive oil.

3 Add the yeast to the bowl of flour and mix the ingredients with your hands to form a dough. Transfer to a lightly floured work surface and knead for 10–12 minutes, until smooth, velvety and elastic. (Alternatively, you can knead the dough in a heavy-duty electric mixer fitted with a dough hook.)

4 Sprinkle on half the paprika and the chopped rosemary and knead briefly to incorporate.

5 Brush a large baking tray with a little olive oil and scatter with some extra flour.

6 Turn the dough onto a work surface and shape it into an oval. Use a rolling pin to roll it out to a rectangle of around 30 x 45 cm, then lift it onto the tray.

7 Cover with a tea towel and leave to rise in a warm place for 1 hour, or until doubled in size.

CONTINUED »

8 Preheat the oven to 180°C.

9 Use your fingertips to make indentations in neat, evenly spaced rows across the surface of the bread.

10 Brush the focaccia with olive oil and sprinkle with the remaining paprika, rosemary leaves and salt flakes.

11 Bake for 10–15 minutes, until golden brown. The base of the loaf should sound hollow when you tap it.

12 Leave to cool on a wire rack. This style of bread is best eaten on the day it's made, but it also reheats well the day after.

Makes 1 large focaccia

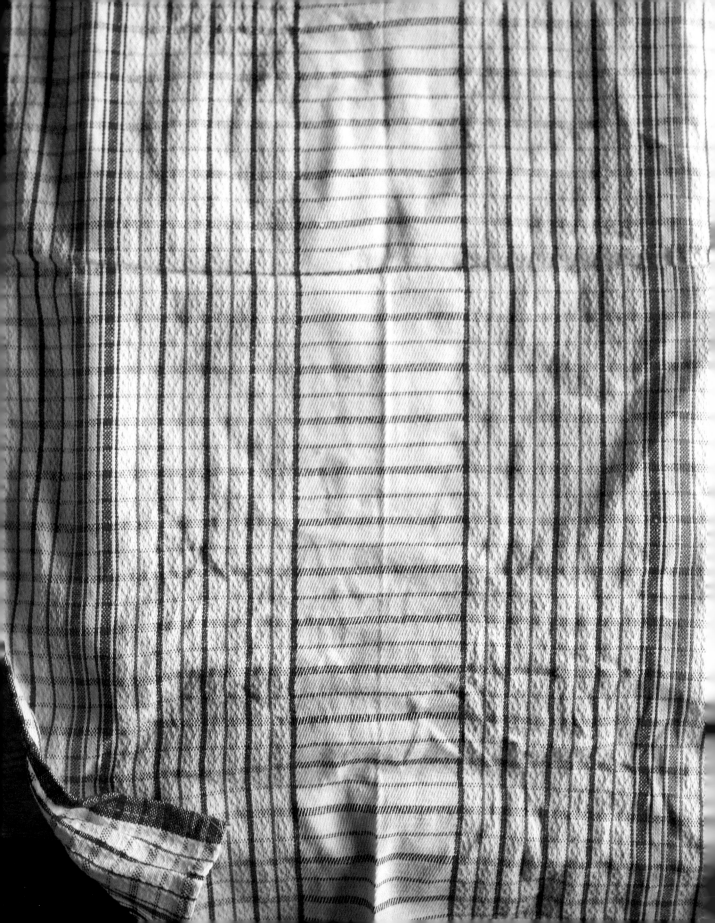

GREEN OLIVE ROLLS

I find these crusty, golden rolls irresistible. It is important to use good-quality green olives; taste them before you buy them to make sure they have a nice flavour and are not too salty.

Whisk the yeast and 2 tablespoons of the warm water in a small bowl and leave for about 10 minutes to activate.

Put the oil, flour and salt in the bowl of a heavy-duty electric mixer fitted with a dough hook. Add the yeast and begin to mix on low speed to combine the ingredients. With the motor going, gradually add the remaining warm water. Mix for 2 minutes, or until the dough is smooth, then add the olives and mix briefly to incorporate. (If you don't have an electric mixer, you can mix the dough by hand.)

Turn the dough out onto a work surface and knead briefly by hand. Return to the bowl, cover with a tea towel and leave to rise in a warm place for $1\frac{1}{2}$–2 hours, or until doubled in size.

Knock the dough back and turn it out onto your work surface. Divide into 12 portions and shape into rolls. Arrange the rolls on a large baking tray dusted with extra flour, cover with a tea towel and leave to rise in a warm place for 20 minutes.

While the rolls are rising, preheat the oven to 220°C. When ready to bake, lower the temperature to 200°C and put the rolls in the oven. Bake for 15–20 minutes or until golden brown. The bases should sound hollow when you tap them. Leave to cool on a wire rack before eating.

Makes 12 rolls

$3\frac{1}{2}$ teaspoons dried yeast or 25 g fresh yeast

310 ml warm water

125 ml olive oil

500 g unbleached strong flour

$1\frac{1}{2}$ teaspoons salt

340 g Sicilian-style green olives, pitted and roughly chopped

POTATO BREAD

This is an old-fashioned recipe first shown to me by my hairdresser and friend, Joyce. It's a rustic loaf with the surprising inclusion of potatoes, not only to add a unique flavour — quite different to normal bread — but to keep the crumb moist and tender.

Boil the potatoes until tender. Drain well and set aside to cool briefly.

Whisk the yeast and warm water in a small bowl and leave for about 10 minutes to activate.

When the potatoes are just cool enough to handle, peel them and push through a potato ricer or food mill into the bowl of a heavy-duty electric mixer. (If you don't have a potato ricer, you can mash them until very smooth and free of lumps.) Work quickly so the potatoes stay warm.

Add the yeast, oil, flour and salt and knead with a dough hook on low speed for 2–3 minutes. Add an extra splash of water if necessary until the dough comes together in a ball and feels slightly sticky. (If you don't have an electric mixer, you can mix the dough by hand.)

Tip the dough onto a lightly floured work surface and knead by hand for 3–4 minutes. Return to the bowl, cover with a tea towel and and leave to rise in a warm place for $1\frac{1}{2}$–2 hours, or until doubled in size.

Knock the dough back and turn it out onto a lightly floured work surface. Use a light touch to shape the dough into a round loaf, then place it on a large baking tray dusted with flour. Cover with a damp tea towel and leave to rise in a warm place for 45 minutes, or until doubled in size.

While the loaf is rising, preheat the oven to 230°C. Heat a pizza stone or tray in the oven. When you are ready to bake, sprinkle the hot stone or tray with semolina and carefully invert the loaf onto it. Bake for 35–40 minutes, spraying the oven with water 3 times during the first 10 minutes. The bread is cooked when it is golden brown and the base sounds hollow when you tap it. Leave to cool on a wire rack before eating.

Makes 1 loaf

675 g waxy potatoes (such as Nicola or roseval)

5 teaspoons dried yeast or 35 g fresh yeast

3 tablespoons warm water

$1\frac{1}{2}$–2 tablespoons olive oil

500 g unbleached strong flour

$1\frac{1}{2}$ teaspoons salt

fine semolina for dusting

PIZZA DOUGH

When I make pizzas at home, I nearly always prepare double the amount of dough — this quantity is enough to make around ten pizzas. Once the dough has risen and been knocked back, you can freeze any you don't need for another occasion.

Whisk the yeast with 50 ml of the warm water and 1 tablespoon of the flour in a small bowl and leave for about 10 minutes to activate.

Put the remaining flour, oil, sugar and salt into the bowl of a heavy-duty electric mixer fitted with a dough hook. Add the yeast and knead on low speed to combine the ingredients. With the motor going, gradually add the remaining warm water until the dough comes together in a ball. Increase the speed and knead for 10 minutes, or until smooth and elastic. (If you don't have an electric mixer, you can knead the dough by hand.) Cover the bowl of dough with a tea towel and leave to rise in a warm place for about 1–1½ hours, until doubled in size.

Preheat the oven to 230°C.

Knock the dough back and turn it out onto a clean work surface. At this stage you can roll the dough out to make pizzas, or wrap any that you don't use in plastic wrap and freeze for another occassion. (When using frozen dough, allow it to come to room temperature slowly, and once defrosted, leave to rise in a warm place for about 30 minutes before rolling out and baking.)

If proceeding straight away, allow the dough to sit for another 10–15 minutes while you preheat the pizza stones (if you have any) or baking tray in the oven. When you are ready to bake, roll the dough out into freeform circles about 1 cm thick. Place on hot pizza stones or trays and cover with your favourite toppings. Bake for 8–10 minutes or until the bases are crisp and golden.

Makes enough for 10 pizzas

15 g dried yeast

300-350 ml warm water

900 g plain flour

3 tablespoons extra-virgin olive oil

1 teaspoon sugar

1 teaspoon salt

TOPPING SUGGESTIONS

Spread a few tablespoons of tomato sauce over the pizza base and top with your favourite ingredients. Some of mine are:

✳ *Fresh tomato, hot salami, basil and buffalo mozzarella*

✳ *Roasted red peppers, sliced onions, salami, anchovies and fresh chillies*

✳ *Mushrooms, prosciutto and truffled pecorino*

✳ *Prawns, ham, rocket, olive oil and roasted garlic.*

Or for a dessert pizza, sprinkle the base with soft brown sugar and bake for 8-10 minutes. When the pizza is crisp, spread with nutella and top with sliced bananas.

WHITE BEAN DIP

I make this dip with all sorts of dried beans, but here I suggest butter beans. If you don't have time to soak and cook the beans yourself, you can use a good-quality tinned variety, although tinned beans need a good rinse or they can taste a bit metallic.

Combine the beans and garlic paste in a food processor and blend until the beans and their skins have completely broken down to form a very smooth paste. Add the lemon juice and cumin and whiz to combine. With the motor still running, drizzle in the oil. Taste and adjust the seasoning to your liking.

If not serving the dip immediately, store in an airtight container in the refrigerator for up to 1 week.

Makes 450 g

400 g cooked butter beans

1 garlic clove, crushed to a paste with 1 teaspoon salt

juice of 2 lemons

pinch of ground cumin

3 tablespoons extra-virgin olive oil

TZATZIKI

Everybody knows this popular and very versatile Greek dip, but it is deliciously thick and creamy when you make it with yoghurt that has been drained overnight to form labne — fresh yoghurt cheese. For how to make labne, see page 66.

Place the cucumber in a colander and sprinkle generously with salt. Leave for 10 minutes (the salt will extract juices from the cucumber), then rinse off the salt and squeeze firmly to extract as much moisture as possible.

Place the cucumber in a mixing bowl and combine with the remaining ingredients. Taste and adjust the seasoning to your liking. If not serving immediately, store in an airtight container in the refrigerator for up to 1 week.

Makes 580 g

2 lebanese cucumbers, grated
salt
400 g soft Labne
juice of 1 lemon
1 garlic clove, crushed to a paste with $\frac{1}{2}$ teaspoon salt
2 tablespoons chopped coriander leaves
1 teaspoon dried mint
$\frac{1}{4}$ teaspoon freshly ground white pepper

SEMI-DRIED TOMATO DIP

Commercially made dips that you buy at the deli are fine for a last-minute get-together, but there is nothing to beat dips that you make yourself at home. This intensely flavoured tomato dip is just wonderful spread onto toasted bagels and topped with slices of avocado and a few basil leaves.

Use good-quality semi-dried tomatoes, or make your own from the summer harvest. To do so, slice ripe tomatoes in half through the core and arrange them cut-side up on a baking tray. Drizzle with a little oil and scatter on a little thyme. Set the oven to its lowest temperature and dry the tomatoes for three to four hours, or as long as overnight, with the oven door slightly ajar.

Blend the tomatoes in a food processor to a smooth puree (although a few chunks won't matter). Add the cream cheese and a good pinch of salt and pepper and blend until smooth. With the motor on low speed, slowly drizzle in the oil. Transfer to a bowl and stir in the chives. If not serving immediately, store in an airtight container in the refrigerator for up to 1 week.

Makes 600 g

300 g semi-dried tomatoes

300 g cream cheese

salt

freshly ground black pepper

3 tablespoons olive oil

3 tablespoons snipped chives

BABA GHANOUSH

My nonna was born and grew up in Egypt, so her cooking always included a few Middle Eastern flavours and techniques alongside her Italian classics. I have very strong memories of her grilling eggplant over the gas burner in her kitchen — always a sure sign that baba ghanoush was being made. To this day, whenever I eat this luscious, smoky, irresistible dip, it transports me back to her kitchen.

For the best flavour, you really should grill the eggplants directly over a gas flame or, ideally, on the barbecue. You can roast them in the oven, but this won't give the authentic smokiness.

Prick the eggplants all over with a fork, then sit them directly on a low–medium flame on your stove. Cook for 10 minutes, turning frequently, until the eggplants are blackened and blistered all over and have collapsed. Remove from the flame and sit them on a small wire rack. Place the whole rack inside a plastic bag and leave the eggplants to steam and cool for 10 minutes. Peel the eggplants, using a small knife to scrape the flesh from the skin if needed.

Chop the flesh roughly and place in a clean tea towel. Tie the corners of the towel together to form a bag and suspend it from a wooden spoon set over a bowl. Allow to drain in the refrigerator overnight.

The next day, tip the eggplant into the bowl of a food processor and add the garlic paste. Whiz briefly to combine. Add the remaining ingredients one at a time and whiz until combined. Taste and adjust the seasoning to your liking.

If not serving the baba ghanoush immediately, store in an airtight container in the refrigerator for up to 1 week.

Makes 1 kg

2 large eggplants

1 garlic clove, crushed to a paste with 1 teaspoon salt

125 g soft Labne (for recipe see page 66)

juice of 3 lemons

75 g tahini

3 tablespoons extra-virgin olive oil

100 ml vegetable oil

freshly ground black pepper

Picnics

AND PARTIES

SMOKED CHICKEN, WATERCRESS AND
MAYONNAISE RIBBON SANDWICHES

MAN-SIZED MEATBALLS STUFFED WITH CHEESE AND HAM

VEGETABLE SAMOSAS WITH MINTED YOGHURT

SAUSAGE ROLLS

PISSALADIÉRE

GOAT'S CHEESE TARTLETS WITH SWEET CAPSICUM

STRAWBERRY SPONGE BIRTHDAY CAKE

RUSSIAN STRAWBERRIES

PLUM AND KIRSCH CAKE

MICHELLE'S TUSCAN CAKE

SIX-LAYER CHOCOLATE CAKE

FOR ME, summer is all about eating outdoors. Everyone loves a picnic, but sometimes it's easy to get bogged down with the same old sandwiches and thermos of tea!

I like to have fun with food on picnics, so this chapter has loads of suggestions for the hamper. For me, ease of transportation and minimal palaver are crucial — and they always are when you've got kids. You want items that you can eat easily with your hands, so you don't have to worry too much about lugging cutlery and plates.

Most of the recipes in this chapter can also do double-duty at parties. Some make great finger food to nibble on with drinks; others will go brilliantly on a table buffet; and I've also included some of my favourite party cakes. And because many kids (and those of us who are kids at heart) have a sweet tooth, I also refer you to Biscuits on page 134 for some great ideas, and to Drinks on page 138 for some child- and adult-friendly summer refreshments.

SMOKED CHICKEN, WATERCRESS AND MAYONNAISE RIBBON SANDWICHES

This is my ideal combo for a picnic sandwich. Here I use smoked chicken, which you can buy at delis, but I sometimes make these sandwiches with fresh chicken breast gently poached in a little water or stock, flavoured with white wine, a bay leaf and a few celery chunks.

It is fairly easy to buy good-quality mayonnaise these days, but I think everyone should know how to make it by hand themselves, as the homemade stuff is just so much better. This version is nice and lemony, but you can add fresh herbs or other flavourings as you wish.

To make the mayonnaise, whisk the egg yolks, mustard, vinegar and lemon juice in a mixing bowl. Add a few drops of the oil and whisk in well, then continue adding the oil in small drizzles. When about a quarter of the oil has been added, you can start increasing the amount you add each time. Continue adding the oil and whisking until all the oil is incorporated. Taste and season to your liking. Transfer to a jar or airtight container and refrigerate until required. The mayonnaise will keep for up to 2 weeks.

Mix the chicken, watercress, parsley and lemon juice with a few tablespoons of the mayonnaise. Season to taste with salt and pepper.

Butter the bread and divide the filling evenly between 6 of the slices, spreading it across the slices. Sit the remaining slices on top and gently squish the sandwiches together. Use a sharp serrated knife — or an electric carving knife is even better — to slice off the crusts. Cut each sandwich into 3 'ribbons' (fingers).

Makes 6 sandwiches

1 smoked chicken breast, finely shredded

2 cups watercress sprigs, roughly chopped

3 tablespoons chopped flat-leaf parsley

juice of $\frac{1}{2}$ lemon

salt

freshly ground black pepper

butter

12 slices of good-quality square bread (white or wholemeal)

Mayonnaise

2 egg yolks

1 tablespoon dijon mustard

1 tablespoon white wine vinegar

juice of $\frac{1}{2}$ lemon

250 ml olive oil or vegetable oil

salt

MAN-SIZED MEATBALLS
STUFFED WITH CHEESE AND HAM

There is nothing fancy or gourmet about these meatballs. They are whoppers, and have a lovely melting, cheesy middle that oozes out when you cut into them. Serve with fried eggs, chips and tomato sauce for a very hearty meal!

Combine the meatball ingredients in a large mixing bowl. Use your hands to squish everything together thoroughly.

In a separate bowl, combine the filling ingredients.

Divide the meatball mixture into 12 portions and roll into smooth, round balls. They will be about the size of a tennis ball. Use your thumb to make a hole in the middle of each meatball and stuff in some of the filling. Seal each meatball around the filling and reshape into a smooth ball.

When ready to cook, heat a little oil in a large frying pan. Fry half the meatballs, turning frequently, until they are well browned and cooked through. They'll take around 8–10 minutes. Drain well on paper towel, then transfer to a low oven to keep warm while you cook the remaining meatballs.

Serves 4–6

1 kg finely minced pork (or beef or lamb)

1 onion, finely diced

3 garlic cloves, crushed

1 tablespoon worcestershire sauce

1 teaspoon tabasco sauce

3 tablespoons chopped flat-leaf parsley

$1\frac{1}{2}$ teaspoons salt

$\frac{1}{2}$ tablespoon freshly ground black pepper

$\frac{1}{2}$ cup breadcrumbs

1 egg, lightly beaten

olive oil for frying

Filling

2 slices of ham, finely chopped

$\frac{1}{2}$ cup grated mozzarella

1 tablespoon finely chopped thyme

$\frac{1}{2}$ teaspoon freshly ground black pepper

VEGETABLE SAMOSAS WITH MINTED YOGHURT

I learnt to love Indian food when I spent time working in an Indian restaurant during my apprenticeship. Later I learnt a whole lot more when I was lucky enough to travel around that crazy, wonderful country, and I still think that Indian cooking is some of the best in the world.

Everyone loves these spicy, crunchy samosas — which can be served piping hot or at room temperature with cool, minted yoghurt.

To make the samosa dough, sift the flour, salt and cumin into a large bowl. Combine the butter and water in a small saucepan and bring to a boil. Tip onto the dry ingredients and use a wooden spoon to mix into a dough. Turn onto a lightly floured work surface and knead gently for 3–4 minutes to form a smooth, slightly elastic dough. Cover with plastic wrap and leave to rest for 30 minutes.

To make the filling, heat 3 tablespoons of vegetable oil in a large heavy-based frying pan. Add the onion and garlic and fry gently for 3–4 minutes, until the onion is soft but not coloured. Add the ginger and fry for another minute. Stir in the garam masala and chilli flakes (if using) and fry for another 2 minutes. Add the vegetables and cook for 6–7 minutes, until the potatoes are beginning to break down. Stir in the lime juice and coriander and season to taste. Remove from the heat and leave to cool.

To make the minted yoghurt, mix the yoghurt with the herbs and lime juice and season to taste with salt and pepper. Refrigerate until ready to serve.

Roll the samosa dough out on a lightly floured work surface to about 3 mm thick. Use a sharp knife to cut out 5 x 15 cm circles, then cut each in half to form 10 semicircles. Working with one semicircle at a time, moisten the straight edge with a little water and wrap the semicircle into a cone, pressing on the outside edge to seal. Spoon in some filling. Moisten the top edges of pastry and fold one side over the other, pressing to seal. Repeat with the remaining pastry and filling.

Pour vegetable oil for deep-frying into a heavy-based saucepan and heat to 180°C. Fry the samosas in batches until crisp and golden brown. Drain briefly on paper towel then enjoy straight away, or allow to cool to room temperature. Serve with minted yoghurt.

Makes 10

240 g plain flour

½ teaspoon salt

½ teaspoon ground cumin, toasted

100 g butter

100 ml water

vegetable oil

1 onion, finely diced

2 garlic cloves, crushed

1 tablespoon grated ginger

1 tablespoon Garam Masala (for recipe see page 302)

1 teaspoon dried chilli flakes (optional)

1 large potato, boiled and cut into 2 cm dice

1 medium carrot, boiled and cut into 1 cm dice

¼ cup peas, blanched

juice of 1 lime

½ cup chopped coriander leaves

salt

freshly ground black pepper

vegetable oil for deep-frying

Minted Yoghurt

250 ml thick natural yoghurt

3 tablespoons chopped mint leaves

3 tablespoons chopped coriander leaves

juice of 1 lime

pinch of salt

pinch of freshly ground black pepper

SAUSAGE ROLLS

The beauty of sausage rolls is that they are delicious hot, warm or cold. You can use good-quality purchased puff pastry if you prefer, but homemade rough puff tastes much, much better, and it isn't hard to make. Serve with good homemade Tomato Relish (page 177).

Combine the filling ingredients in a large mixing bowl. Use your hands to squish everything together thoroughly.

Roll the pastry out on a lightly floured work surface to form a very large rectangle, about 45 cm long and 20 cm wide. Cut into 2 x 10 cm wide strips and trim the ends neatly. Divide the filling between each strip and form into a long sausage along the centre. Roll the pastry around the filling and seal the edge by brushing it with the beaten egg before pressing down with a fork. Cover and refrigerate for 1 hour, or longer if more convenient.

Preheat the oven to 200°C and lightly oil a baking tray. Cut each log into 4 cm slices and arrange on the tray. Lightly brush the tops with more beaten egg and bake for 15–20 minutes, or until golden brown.

Serve hot from the oven or at room temperature, with plenty of tomato relish.

Makes 24 mini rolls

500 g Rough Puff Pastry (for recipe see page 296)

1 egg, lightly beaten

Filling

500 g minced beef

1 medium carrot, grated

1 small onion, very finely diced

1 garlic clove, crushed

2 tablespoons worcestershire sauce

3 tablespoons chopped flat-leaf parsley

2 tablespoons dijon mustard

3 tablespoons breadcrumbs

PISSALADIÈRE

A French classic, this onion and anchovy tart is perfect for picnics, parties or as a snack. It's usually made on puff pastry but works just as well on a pizza base, or even on crunchy, golden filo. I think this is my favourite version, though, using a meltingly crisp, short pastry that's dead-easy to make. The secret ingredient in the pastry is yoghurt, which sets off the sweetness of the onion topping brilliantly. (This recipe makes double the quantity of pastry needed, but you can freeze the rest and whip it out on another occasion.)

The components of the tart can be made ahead of time and put together quickly just before you are ready to serve. It makes a lovely lunch dish or starter for a dinner party with a simple green leaf salad as the accompaniment.

To make the pastry, sift the flour and salt onto a work surface. Make a well in the centre and pour in the beaten egg. Use your fingers to gradually work the egg into the flour. Add the yoghurt and continue to work in with your hands until incorporated into a very soft dough. Knead gently until smooth. Divide in half and wrap both pieces in plastic wrap. Refrigerate one piece for at least 1 hour before rolling, and freeze the other piece for another occasion (it can be frozen for up to 3 months).

Roll the pastry out to a 20 x 30 cm rectangle. Lift onto a lightly oiled baking tray and refrigerate for another hour.

To prepare the topping, heat the olive oil in a large heavy-based frying pan. Add the onions and thyme and cook over low heat for 15–20 minutes, until very soft and golden brown. Remove from the heat and leave to cool.

Preheat the oven to 200°C and bake the pastry rectangle for 20–25 minutes, or until crisp and golden brown. Remove from the oven and leave to cool.

To assemble the tart, spread the onions out over the pastry base. Arrange the capsicum strips in diagonal rows over the surface. Arrange the anchovies in diagonal rows crisscrossing the capsicum, forming large diamond shapes. Sit a halved olive in the middle of each diamond. Drizzle on a little extra-virgin olive oil and serve straight away.

Serves 4

Yoghurt Pastry

600 g plain flour

pinch of salt

1 egg, lightly beaten

500 g yoghurt

Topping

3 tablespoons olive oil

4 large onions, very finely sliced

1 tablespoon chopped thyme

2 red capsicums, roasted, peeled, seeded and cut into thin strips

20 anchovy fillets

150 g black olives, pitted and halved

extra-virgin olive oil for drizzling

GOAT'S CHEESE TARTLETS WITH SWEET CAPSICUM

Brilliant for picnics, these tartlets are also great for cocktail parties. Serve with a dollop of Tomato Relish (page 177), Tomato and Chive Salsa (page 84) or Salsa Verde (page 27).

To make the pastry, combine the flour, salt and butter in a food processor and blitz to sandy crumbs. Lightly beat the egg with the egg yolks and add to the flour mixture. Pulse until incorporated. With the motor running, slowly drizzle in the water until the mixture starts to come together in a ball. Tip onto a lightly floured work surface and knead briefly until smooth. Cover in plastic wrap and refrigerate for at least 1 hour before rolling. You'll need around 600 g of pastry to make the tartlets, so the rest can be stored in the refrigerator for up to 4 days or in the freezer for up to 3 months.

Roll the pastry out on a lightly floured work surface to about 3 mm thick. (You might find it easier to work with half the dough at a time.) Cut out 24 x 7 cm circles with a sharp knife or pastry cutter (a fluted cutter gives a decorative edge). Brush 2 x 12-hole cupcake trays lightly with oil and line with the pastry circles. Refrigerate for 30 minutes.

Preheat the oven to 180°C. In a large mixing bowl, whisk the eggs with the cream, salt, pepper and nutmeg. Divide the capsicum, goat's cheese, herbs and olives between the tarts, then carefully pour in the egg and cream mixture, filling to just beneath the pastry rim.

Bake for 12–15 minutes, until the pastry is golden brown and the filling is just set. Allow the tartlets to cool in the trays before carefully removing them. Serve at room temperature.

Makes 24

Shortcrust Pastry

Shortcrust Pastry

500 g plain flour

pinch of salt

300 g butter, roughly chopped

1 egg plus 2 egg yolks

2 tablespoons water

Filling

5 eggs

250 ml pure cream

1 teaspoon salt

$\frac{1}{2}$ teaspoon freshly ground black pepper

pinch of ground nutmeg

1 large red capsicum, roasted, peeled, seeded and chopped

100 g goat's cheese, cut into 1 cm dice

3 tablespoons chopped basil leaves

2 tablespoons chopped flat-leaf parsley

60 g green olives, pitted and roughly chopped

STRAWBERRY SPONGE BIRTHDAY CAKE

This is my sons' favourite celebration cake. It can be as simple or as fancy and multi-layered as you like. I use homemade jam (or good-quality bought jam), lots of cream and tip-top summer strawberries.

Preheat the oven to 180°C. Butter a 25 cm cake tin and line the base and sides with baking paper.

Beat the egg whites to thick, stiff peaks and set aside.

Beat the egg yolks, sugar and vanilla seeds until very pale, thick and creamy. Add the warm melted butter and sift on the flour, but do not stir yet. Now add a third of the egg whites and use a whisk to fold everything together gently but thoroughly. Fold in the rest of the egg whites.

Gently spoon the batter into the prepared tin and bake for 40 minutes, or until a skewer comes out clean. Allow the cake to cool in the tin for a few minutes, then invert onto a wire rack and leave to cool completely.

Whip the cream with the sugar. Mix the strawberry jam with the brandy, if using. Slice the sponge in half and spread the bottom with the jam and a thin layer of whipped cream. Add the top of the sponge and spread the top and sides with the remaining cream. Decorate with the strawberries.

Serves 8–10

6 eggs, separated

175 g caster sugar

$\frac{1}{4}$ vanilla pod, seeds scraped

90 g unsalted butter, melted

150 g self-raising flour

Filling

400 ml cream

2 tablespoons caster sugar

$\frac{1}{2}$ cup good-quality strawberry jam

a few tablespoons of brandy (optional)

500 g ripe strawberries, hulled but left whole

RUSSIAN STRAWBERRIES

Make this simple but effective summer dessert when strawberries are at their best. Omit the vodka if making this for kids.

Combine the strawberries, sugar, vanilla seeds and vodka in a bowl and leave to macerate for 1 hour.

Mix the clotted cream with the sour cream, then spoon on top of the strawberries. For an extra indulgence, sprinkle on brown sugar and leave for 5 minutes to dissolve into a lovely layer of soft toffee.

Serves 4

500 g ripe strawberries, hulled and cut in half

2 tablespoons caster sugar

½ vanilla pod, seeds scraped

125 ml vodka

200 ml clotted cream

2 tablespoons sour cream

⅓ cup brown sugar (optional)

PLUM AND KIRSCH CAKE

Now is the time to confess that I stole this recipe from my mother-in-law! She can sometimes be a little bit guarded about sharing her recipes. It took a lot of sneaking around to find this one, I can tell you, but it is such a good cake that I felt it was worth the risk. Thanks Oma!

Toss the plums with the kirsch and brown sugar and set aside for at least 1 hour.

Preheat the oven to 180°C and butter a 26 or 27 cm springform cake tin.

Cream the butter and sugar until light and fluffy. Add the eggs one at a time and beat well. Sift the flour and baking powder into a separate bowl, then fold into the butter mixture. Pour into the tin and smooth the surface. Arrange the plums cut-side up on top of the cake, reserving the leftover kirsch syrup. Bake the cake for 1 hour, or until a skewer comes out clean.

Remove the cake from the oven and drizzle with the kirsch syrup. Allow to cool in the tin for about 30 minutes, then remove from the tin and leave to cool completely.

Serve plain with a cup of coffee, or as a dessert with lots of whipped cream.

Serves 8–10

800 g plums, halved and stoned

125 ml kirsch (cherry brandy)

40 g brown sugar

250 g unsalted butter at room temperature

250 g caster sugar

4 eggs

400 g self-raising flour

1 teaspoon baking powder

MICHELLE'S TUSCAN CAKE

My gorgeous wife Michelle made this cake for me when we were first dating. She has always known that the way to a man's heart is through his stomach! It is quick to make, and stays moist for days — although it's unlikely to last that long.

Preheat the oven to 180°C. Grease and line a 26 cm cake tin.

To make the topping, combine the butter, sugar, liquid glucose and water in a saucepan and heat gently until melted. Stir in the currants, almonds and pine nuts.

Meanwhile, combine the butter and sugar in the bowl of an electric mixer and cream until pale and fluffy. Add the eggs, one at a time making sure each is thoroughly incorporated before adding the next. Fold in the ground almonds, followed by the flour. Gently fold in half the topping mixture then spoon the batter into the prepared cake tin and bake for 30 minutes.

Once the cake has been in the oven for 30 minutes, pour on the rest of the topping mixture and return to the oven. Increase the temperature to 200°C and bake for a further 10 minutes.

Remove from the oven and allow to cool in the tin for a few minutes before turning out onto a wire rack.

Serves 8–10

240 g unsalted butter at room temperature

480 g caster sugar

6 eggs

480 g ground almonds

120 g plain flour, sifted

Topping

180 g unsalted butter

180 g caster sugar

180 g liquid glucose

90 ml water

100 g currants

200 g flaked almonds

150 g pine nuts

SIX-LAYER CHOCOLATE CAKE

Whoever says you can have too much of a good thing hasn't tried this cake! It is a chocolate extravaganza with layers of dense, chocolatey cake sandwiched with rich, chocolatey filling. It might be a bit messy to take on a picnic, but it's an ace party cake! Please use good-quality dark chocolate.

Melt the chocolate in a bowl set over a saucepan of simmering water. Leave to cool to room temperature.

Preheat the oven to 165°C. Butter 3 x 23 cm cake tins and line them with baking paper.

Cream the butter and sugar with electric beaters until pale and fluffy. With the beaters on low speed, add the crème fraîche and vanilla and mix until combined. Sift the flour, baking powder and salt into a separate bowl, then mix into the butter mixture in small batches alternating with the eggs. When all the flour and eggs are incorporated, add the cooled melted chocolate and mix in slowly. Pour into the tins and bake for 45–50 minutes, or until a skewer comes out clean. Leave the cakes to cool in the tins for 10 minutes, then invert onto wire racks and leave to cool completely.

To make the frosting, melt the chocolate in a bowl set over a saucepan of simmering water. Leave to cool to room temperature.

Beat the cream cheese and butter together until smooth. Add the icing sugar and cocoa and beat again until smooth. Add the cooled melted chocolate and mix in slowly.

Carefully slice each cake in half horizontally. Spread a generous layer of frosting on one half and top with another, pressing together gently but firmly. Continue spreading frosting and stacking on cake until you have used all the cake, but not all the frosting. Spread the remaining frosting around the sides and over the top of the cake. Serve alone or with fresh summer berries.

Serves 8–10

600 g good-quality dark chocolate, roughly chopped

450 g unsalted butter at room temperature

600 g caster sugar

230 g crème fraîche

1 tablespoon vanilla extract

450 g self-raising flour

1 teaspoon baking powder

1 teaspoon salt

9 large eggs

Chocolate and Cream Cheese Frosting

650 g good-quality dark chocolate, roughly chopped

400 g cream cheese at room temperature

500 g unsalted butter at room temperature

500 g icing sugar, sifted

60 g cocoa, sifted

Biscuits

NONNA'S SHORTBREAD CRESCENTS

Nonna used to make these shortbreads in vast quantities at Christmas, but they are perfect at any time of year, especially served with a strong Italian espresso. The recipe makes around eighty crescents, as Nonna wouldn't think it worth making a smaller quantity as she knew how quickly they would be gobbled up. However, the dough freezes well if you would prefer to cook less; that way, you can quickly defrost it and bake another batch when you feel like it.

Cream the butter, sugar and vanilla with electric beaters until light and fluffy. Beat in the eggs one at a time, then fold in the flours. Add the honey and rosewater and mix to a smooth, stiff dough.

Tip the dough onto a work surface and divide into quarters. Roll each piece into a long rope about 1 cm thick. Cut into 4 cm lengths and shape into crescents, pinching the ends to form points. Arrange on trays lined with baking paper and refrigerate for 10 minutes.

Preheat the oven to 160°C. Bake the crescents for 10–12 minutes, until just beginning to colour a pale gold. Transfer to a wire rack and dust generously with icing sugar while still warm, then leave to cool. Store in an airtight container with more icing sugar. They should keep for up to 1 week.

Makes around 80

250 g unsalted butter at room temperature

150 g caster sugar

$\frac{1}{4}$ teaspoon vanilla extract

2 eggs

400 g plain flour, sifted

100 g cornflour, sifted

2 tablespoons honey, warmed

1 tablespoon rosewater

200 g icing sugar

ANZAC BISCUITS

Every Aussie and Kiwi kid loves an Anzac biscuit; they just seem to be part of our psyche. They are also delicious in a lovely, crunchy ice cream (for recipe see page 143).

150 g plain flour, sifted
100 g rolled oats
80 g desiccated coconut
150 g caster sugar
125 g unsalted butter
85 g golden syrup
5 teaspoons bicarbonate of soda, sifted
1 tablespoon boiling water

Preheat the oven to 160°C. Combine the flour, oats, coconut and sugar in a large mixing bowl.

Place the butter and golden syrup in a saucepan and melt over medium heat. Stir well, then turn off the heat and allow to cool a little.

Combine the bicarbonate of soda and boiling water in a small bowl, then add to the melted butter and syrup. Pour into the dry ingredients and stir well with a wooden spoon.

Place large spoonfuls of mixture onto trays lined with baking paper. Leave about 5 cm between each spoonful as the biscuits spread while cooking. Use your fingers to flatten them a little bit.

Bake for 10 minutes, or until golden brown. Transfer to a wire rack to cool.

Makes 10–12 large biscuits

EXTRA-CHOCOLATEY COOKIES

These are brilliant with a scoop of vanilla ice cream, or just with a cup of tea. You can vary the recipe by using milk or white chocolate if you prefer.

Melt 120 g of the chocolate in a bowl set over a saucepan of simmering water. Leave to cool to room temperature.

Preheat the oven to 160°C. Cream the butter and sugar with electric beaters until the sugar has dissolved and the mixture is fluffy. Beat in the cooled melted chocolate, then the egg and vanilla.

Sift the flour, cocoa, bicarbonate of soda and salt into a separate bowl, then add to the chocolate mixture and mix to a smooth dough. Stir in the remaining chopped chocolate.

Roll into walnut-sized balls and arrange on trays lined with baking paper, leaving plenty of space between the balls as they spread while cooking. Press the balls down with the back of a fork and bake for 10–12 minutes. Transfer to a wire rack to cool.

Makes 32

400 g dark chocolate, roughly chopped

110 g unsalted butter at room temperature

120 g brown sugar

1 egg

1 teaspoon vanilla extract

80 g plain flour

35 g cocoa

1 teaspoon bicarbonate of soda

½ teaspoon salt

HONEY BISCUITS

Nearly everyone I know loves these biscuits, and I find they will settle even the most unruly child — for up to ten minutes if you are lucky! I like them best with a cup of herbal tea.

The dough is formed into a log and chilled before being sliced and baked — it can also be frozen for up to three months, so you can slice discs off whenever you feel like knocking up a few biscuits.

Cream the butter and honey with electric beaters until light and fluffy, then beat in the egg. Add the remaining ingredients and mix to a smooth, firm dough.

Tip the dough onto a work surface and roll into a short, fat log. Wrap tightly in plastic wrap and refrigerate overnight, until really firm.

Preheat the oven to 160°C and line a tray with baking paper. Cut the dough into 1 cm slices and arrange on the tray leaving some space in between the slices.

Bake for 8–10 minutes, until golden brown. Transfer to a wire rack to cool.

Makes 12 large biscuits

170 g unsalted butter at room temperature

145 ml honey, warmed

1 egg

285 g plain flour

grated zest of 1 lemon and juice of $\frac{1}{2}$ lemon

pinch of salt

pinch of ground cloves

Drinks

GINGER BEER

There's nothing to beat a long glass of homemade, mouth-tingling ginger beer on a hot summer's day. It's really refreshing and goes brilliantly with spicy Asian food.

100 g ginger, grated
½ cup brown sugar
juice of 1 lemon
1 cinnamon stick

250 ml water
ice
soda water
mint sprigs

Combine the ginger, sugar, lemon juice and cinnamon in a jug and stir until the sugar dissolves. Stir in the water, then cover and refrigerate for 4 days to allow the flavours to develop.

Strain and pour into tall glasses with ice. Add soda water to taste (a 4:1 ratio is about right), garnish with mint and serve straight away.

Serves 6

RASPBERRY LEMONADE

My kids really love this lemonade as a treat in summer. It's best when raspberries are at their peak and abundant in the markets, but in truth, it's also pretty good made from frozen raspberries.

500 g fresh or frozen raspberries
220 g sugar

375 ml water
ice
soda water

Combine the raspberries, sugar and water in a saucepan and heat gently until the sugar dissolves, then increase the heat and bring to a boil. Once boiling, remove from the heat. Tip into a blender and whiz to a puree. Push through a fine sieve to remove the seeds, then leave to cool completely.

Pour into tall glasses with ice. Add soda water to taste (a 4:1 ratio is about right) and serve straight away.

Serves 8–10

DIRTY MOJITO

One of the most popular drinks around, a mojito is the classic Cuban cocktail and its sweet-and-sour flavours have kept me going on many a long summer's night.

3 limes, cut into wedges (reserve 2 to garnish)

2 tablespoons brown sugar

1 cup mint leaves, and

2 mint sprigs to garnish

120 ml dark rum (I like the Havana Club range)

crushed ice

soda water

Traditionally, mojitos are made with white Cuban rum and cane sugar, but I like the look and taste of dark rum and brown sugar, which is what makes it 'dirty'. Beware, these are addictive!

Use the end of a rolling pin to 'muddle' (bash) the lime wedges, sugar and mint leaves in a jug or cocktail shaker. Pour in the rum and stir briefly to dissolve the sugar. Divide between 2 tall glasses and fill with crushed ice. Top up with soda water and garnish with the reserved lime wedges and mint sprigs.

Serves 2

CAESAR VODKA

The beauty of vodka is that it takes on other flavours brilliantly, and I always have a couple of bottles in my freezer infused with various aromatics or spices. This spicy vodka makes a great base for cocktails.

750 ml bottle of your favourite vodka

$\frac{1}{4}$ red capsicum, finely sliced

$\frac{1}{2}$ onion, finely sliced

$\frac{1}{3}$ garlic clove, quartered

2 bay leaves

1 long red chilli

5 black peppercorns

handful of flat-leaf parsley

Pour 200 ml of the vodka into a jug and set aside. Push the flavourings into the bottle, then top up with vodka from the jug. You may find there is a small amount left over, which you will have to find some other immediate use for!

Seal the lid tightly and refrigerate for at least 1 week before using to make a vodka martini or bloody mary.

Makes 750 ml

Ice Cream

& FROZEN DESSERTS

CLASSIC VANILLA ICE CREAM

SOUR CREAM ICE CREAM

ANZAC CRUNCH ICE CREAM

RICH CHOCOLATE ICE CREAM

CHRISTMAS PUDDING ICE CREAM

BOMBE ALASKA

PEACH AND AMARETTO SEMIFREDDO

COFFEE GRANITA DUO

CLASSIC VANILLA ICE CREAM

Vanilla ice cream is delicious on its own — perhaps with a big bowl of fresh summer berries, or a drizzle of Chocolate Sauce (for recipe see page 316) — but you can also use it as a base for other ice creams including my very favourite, Anzac Crunch (see opposite).

Combine the cream, milk, vanilla pod and seeds and half the sugar in a large heavy-based saucepan. Heat gently until the sugar dissolves, then increase the heat and bring to just below a simmer, then remove the pan from the heat.

Put the egg yolks and the rest of the sugar in a mixing bowl and beat until light and foamy (use a whisk attachment if you have an electric mixer). With the motor on low speed, add a little of the hot cream mixture, then slowly pour in the rest. Return the mixture to the rinsed-out saucepan and stir continuously over a low heat for 5–10 minutes until the mixture thickens enough to coat the back of the spoon. If you have a sugar thermometer, the mixture should reach 65–70°C.

Strain back into the rinsed-out mixing bowl set over a larger bowl (or sink) of iced water and allow to cool. Fish out the vanilla pod and scrape any remaining seeds into the custard.

When the custard is cold, pour into an ice cream machine and churn according to the manufacturer's instructions. Transfer to an airtight container and store in the freezer for up to 1 month.

Makes 1.25 litres

500 ml cream

500 ml full-cream milk

1 vanilla pod, seeds scraped

250 g sugar

10 egg yolks

SOUR CREAM ICE CREAM

My clever pastry chef Liana Crothers came up with this recipe as a way of dealing with a huge amount of sour cream ordered by mistake. It turned out to be a real winner: tangy and refreshing and dead-easy to make as there's no need to cook up a custard base.

Whisk the ingredients together in a large mixing bowl. Cover and refrigerate overnight.

Pour into an ice cream machine and churn according to the manufacturer's instructions. Transfer to an airtight container and store in the freezer for up to 1 month.

Makes 1.25 litres

500 ml sour cream

375 ml full-cream milk

250 ml cream

730 g caster sugar

2 tablespoons lemon juice

1 tablespoon liquid glucose

$\frac{1}{2}$ vanilla pod, seeds scraped

ANZAC CRUNCH ICE CREAM

The oaty, toffee sweetness of Anzac biscuits adds an irresistible crunch to vanilla ice cream.

Make the vanilla ice cream as described on page 142, and churn according to the manufacturer's instructions. Add the crumbled biscuits towards the end of the churning. Transfer to an airtight container and store in the freezer for up to 1 month.

Makes 1.5 litres

1.25 litres Classic Vanilla Ice Cream (see opposite)

$1\frac{1}{2}$ cups roughly crumbled Anzac Biscuits (for recipe see page 135)

RICH CHOCOLATE ICE CREAM

Wickedly rich, this ice cream is perhaps best reserved for grown-ups. The better the chocolate, the better the ice cream.

Make the vanilla ice cream as described on page 142. Add the chocolate to the thickened hot custard, stirring until completely melted, before returning the custard to the mixing bowl set over iced water.

When the custard is cold, pour into an ice cream machine and churn according to the manufacturer's instructions. Transfer to an airtight container and store in the freezer for up to 1 month.

Makes 1.5 litres

1.25 litres Classic Vanilla Ice Cream (page 142)

750 g dark chocolate, roughly chopped

CHRISTMAS PUDDING ICE CREAM

Sometimes I'm just defeated by the very thought of a hot dessert after a big Italian Christmas dinner. It's times like these that you need Christmas pudding ice cream! It's well suited to warm Australian Christmases, of course, but actually I think it works just as well in winter in the northern hemisphere.

Make the vanilla ice cream as described on page 142, and churn according to the manufacturer's instructions. Add the crumbled plum pudding and brandy towards the end of the churning. Transfer to an airtight container and store in the freezer for up to 1 month.

Makes 1.5 litres

1.25 litres Classic Vanilla Ice Cream (page 142)

600 g good-quality plum pudding, crumbled

3 tablespoons good-quality brandy

BOMBE ALASKA

A knock-out dessert that never fails to impress, and can be prepared ahead of time. You can use any combination of ice cream flavours — I've used vanilla and chocolate here — and to make life easy, use a good-quality purchased sponge cake (although you will find a recipe on page 310). All that leaves, then, is the Italian meringue, which sounds a bit daunting, but is really just about being organised. Have your egg whites ready to go and you will find it quite straightforward.

To make the Italian meringue, put the egg whites in the bowl of an electric mixer and set aside. Put the sugar and glucose in a heavy-based saucepan with just enough water to dampen it. Cook over medium–high heat without stirring — the sugar will gradually dissolve before coming to a boil. Use a pastry brush dipped in water to brush down any crystallised sugar from the sides of the pan so it doesn't burn. As the sugar cooks, check the temperature with a thermometer and when it reaches 118°C (soft-ball stage), begin whisking the egg whites at medium speed.

Whisk the egg whites until they form soft peaks. By this stage, the sugar should have reached 120°C. Remove from the heat, and with the egg whites whisking on low speed, drizzle in the hot syrup. Increase the speed of the mixer and whisk for 12–15 minutes, until the meringue cools completely. It should be smooth, shiny and white. Spoon into a piping bag and refrigerate until ready to serve (it should be used within a day).

To assemble the bombe, lightly oil a 2-litre mould. Cut a disc of sponge to fit the base of the mould snugly. Spoon in vanilla ice cream to halfway up the mould, smooth the surface, and freeze for 30 minutes. Fill with the chocolate ice cream to just below the rim of the mould. Top with another disc of sponge cake and return to the freezer until you are ready to serve.

To unmould the bombe, dip the base of the mould in hot water for 10 seconds, then invert onto a serving plate. Pipe meringue all over the bombe — it doesn't have to be pretty; the wilder it looks, the better.

Warm the brandy (if using) gently (10–15 seconds in a microwave should do), then transfer to a ladle. Light it carefully with a match and drizzle it over the meringue, to brown as much of the surface as you can. Alternatively, singe the meringue all over with a domestic blow torch. Serve straight away with blackberry sauce, or just on its own.

Serves 8

1 good-quality sponge cake, sliced in half

750 g Classic Vanilla Ice Cream (page 142)

750 g Rich Chocolate Ice Cream (page 145)

3 tablespoons good-quality brandy (optional)

Blackberry Sauce (page 310) to serve (optional)

Italian Meringue

10 egg whites (around 350 g)

700 g caster sugar

1 generous tablespoon liquid glucose

PEACH AND AMARETTO SEMIFREDDO

Semifreddos — or parfaits — are a great option if you don't have an ice cream machine. They are a bit like a frozen mousse, and you can make them in all sorts of fancy moulds. The easiest, though, is a terrine mould, and then you serve the semifreddo in slices.

For an impressive effect, make individual semifreddos in small ramekins lined with a band of baking paper that rises at least 5 centimetres above the rim. You remove the paper just before serving and the semifreddos look just like hot baked soufflés.

Line a 1-litre terrine mould with plastic wrap and chill in the freezer.

Combine the peaches with half the sugar and all of the water in a heavy-based saucepan and heat gently until the sugar dissolves, then increase the heat and simmer for 4–6 minutes, or until the peaches are soft. Remove from the heat and leave to cool slightly.

Blitz the peaches in batches in a food processor to make a smooth puree. Push through a fine sieve to remove skin and fibres, then stir in half the amaretto. Refrigerate until chilled.

Whip the cream to soft peaks and refrigerate.

Combine the egg yolks with the remaining sugar and amaretto in a bowl set over a saucepan of simmering water; the base of the bowl should not come in contact with the water. Heat gently, whisking continuously, until the mixture begins to thicken. If you have a sugar thermometer, the mixture should reach about 70°C. Tip into a cool bowl and beat or whisk on medium speed until the mixture cools to room temperature and is pale and creamy. It should be thick enough to form a ribbon that leaves a trail across the surface.

Fold in the chilled peach puree, followed by the whipped cream. Pour into the prepared mould and freeze overnight, or for up to 3 weeks. Remove from the freezer 5–10 minutes before serving. Dip the base of the mould in hot water for 5–10 seconds, then invert onto a serving platter, lifting away the mould and plastic wrap. Use a sharp knife to slice the semifreddo and serve straight away garnished with fresh peach segments, sprigs of mint and extra drizzles of amaretto.

Serves 8

500 g peaches, stoned and roughly chopped, plus extra segments to serve

300 g caster sugar

125 ml water

120 ml amaretto, plus extra to serve

500 ml cream

6 egg yolks

mint sprigs to serve

COFFEE GRANITA DUO

Granitas are brilliantly refreshing, and you don't need any fancy equipment to make them — just a freezer and a shallow container. Serve these elegant granitas instead of coffee after dinner on a hot summer's night.

To make the espresso granita, stir the sugar into the hot coffee until it dissolves. Leave to cool, then pour into a shallow container and freeze.

To make the cafe latte granita, combine the milk and sugar in a saucepan and heat gently until the sugar dissolves. Remove from the heat and leave to cool. Stir in the cooled coffee, pour into a shallow container and freeze.

Every hour or so, take the containers out of the freezer and beat lightly with a fork to mix the frozen crystals into the liquid. By the time you have beaten the granitas several times and they are frozen firm, the texture should be quite granular and icy.

To serve, divide the espresso granita between chilled glasses. Top with the cafe latte granita. Pour a shot of Frangelico over each if desired and serve straight away.

Serves 4

Espresso Granita

150 g sugar

500 ml hot strong coffee

Cafe Latte Granita

500 ml milk

150 g sugar

200 ml strong coffee, cooled

Frangelico to serve (optional)

Jams

NONNA'S APRICOT JAM

Nonna didn't mess around with sugar thermometers and she made the best, most intense apricot jam I've ever tasted. Her recipe is really easy. You just cook the apricots and sugar down to a thick, sticky puree. The kernels add a subtle almond flavour, which combines with the cloves and cardamom to really bring out the flavour of the apricots.

You can use the same recipe to make plum jam, substituting a cinnamon stick for the cloves and cardamom.

Put the sugar in a metal bowl or a baking dish and heat in a 120°C oven for 20–30 minutes.

Put the apricots in a heavy-based pot. Crack the reserved stones to extract the kernels, and add to the apricots with the cloves, cardamom pods and warm sugar. Cook over low heat until the sugar dissolves, then increase the heat and boil for 1 hour, stirring frequently. Remove from the heat and leave to cool a little. Ladle into sterilised jars, distributing the apricot kernels and spices evenly, then seal and store in a cool, dark place.

Makes 1.5 litres

2 kg sugar

3 kg apricots, halved and stoned (reserve a handful of stones)

4 cloves

2 cardamom pods

JOHNNY'S STRAWBERRY JAM

My stepdad is a fanatical jam maker (amongst other things). This is his recipe for a good, easy jam for beginners because the pectin makes it virtually foolproof.

Put the sugar in a metal bowl or a baking dish and heat in a 120°C oven for 20–30 minutes.

Put the strawberries, pectin, cinnamon stick and water in large heavy-based saucepan and bring to a simmer over low heat.

Tip in the warm sugar and cook, stirring, until the sugar dissolves. Increase the heat and boil until the jam reaches setting point at 105°C on a sugar thermometer. (You can also check by putting a spoonful onto a chilled plate and refrigerating for a few minutes — when you tilt the plate the jam shouldn't run.)

Remove from the heat and leave to cool a little. Skim away any froth or scum from the surface and ladle into sterilised jars. Seal and store in a cool, dark place.

Makes 500 ml

500 g sugar
1 kg ripe strawberries, hulled
50 g pectin
1 cinnamon stick
125 ml water

FIG PASTE

In Melbourne, we are lucky enough to have figs in abundance by the end of summer. They are plentiful at the market, and it seems as if everyone has a fig tree in their backyard. This paste is a variation of quince paste, and it's a great way to use up figs that are less than perfect. Serve it the same way as you would quince paste — on a cheese board — or add a dollop to stews or gravies to add a fruity flavour.

The recipe calls for a fairly large amount of figs, but as the paste is the same amount of effort regardless of how much you make, my logic is that you may as well make a decent quantity. If you have a fig tree, build up a store of figs in the freezer until you have enough.

Remove the stalks from the figs and blitz them in batches in a food processor to make a puree.

Put the sugar in a heavy-based pot. Heat gently, stirring frequently, until the sugar dissolves. Increase the heat and cook until the sugar reaches 140°C on a sugar thermometer.

Carefully add the fig puree, lemon juice and vanilla pieces and stir well with your hand wrapped in a tea towel, as the mixture is likely to bubble and spit. Cook over very low heat, stirring frequently, for about 1½ hours, until the mixture comes away from the sides of the pan as a thick paste. Stirring becomes quite hard, but you need to do so frequently towards the end to make sure the paste doesn't stick to the bottom of the pot and burn. When cooked, remove from the heat and allow to cool a little.

Preheat the oven to 50°C. Lightly oil a shallow 18 x 28 cm tray and line it with baking paper. Pour the paste into the tray and smooth it out evenly. Bake overnight, or for a minimum of 8 hours. The paste should become firm and solid.

Transfer to an airtight container (cut if needed) and store in the refrigerator, where it will keep indefinitely.

Makes 1.25 kg

2 kg figs
1 kg caster sugar
juice of 2 lemons
1 vanilla pod, roughly chopped

CHUNKY ORANGE MARMALADE

A blissfully easy marmalade with no peeling or shredding required!

Combine the oranges, spices and water in a heavy-based pot. Bring to a boil, then lower the heat and simmer, covered, for about 1 hour, or until the oranges are very soft and easily pierced with a fork.

Lift the oranges out with a slotted spoon, allowing the liquid to drain back into the pot.

Cut the oranges into quarters and remove all the pips. Cut each quarter into 4–5 small chunks.

Add the sugar to the pot of poaching liquid and heat gently to dissolve. Once dissolved, bring to a boil, then lower the heat and simmer for 5–6 minutes, skimming away any impurities that rise to the surface. Add the pectin and the orange chunks and stir well.

Boil for 30 minutes, stirring regularly. The marmalade should reach setting point by the time it gets to 105°C on a sugar thermometer. (You can also check by putting a spoonful onto a chilled plate and refrigerating for a few minutes — when you tilt the plate the jam shouldn't run.)

Remove from the heat and leave to cool a little. Skim away any froth or scum from the surface and ladle into sterilised jars. Seal tightly and store in a cool, dark place.

Makes 2 litres

2 kg oranges
2 cardamom pods
2 cloves
1 cinnamon stick
2 litres water
2 kg sugar
100 g pectin

Masterclass

HOW TO MAKE TOMATO PASSATA

100 ml olive oil

1 onion, finely diced

3 garlic cloves, finely sliced

3 kg ripe roma tomatoes, roughly chopped

big handful of basil leaves

1 tablespoon sugar

1 tablespoon salt

1 teaspoon freshly ground black pepper

SERVING SUGGESTIONS

No kitchen is complete without passata. Use as a base for simple pasta sauces, braises, soups and even curries.

1 Thoroughly wash 3 x 750 ml bottles together with their lids and leave to air-dry.

2 Heat the oil in a pot. Add the onion and garlic and sweat over low heat for 3–4 minutes, until the onion is soft but not coloured.

3 Add the tomatoes, a few of the basil leaves, and the sugar, salt and pepper. Bring to a boil, then remove from the heat.

4 Working with a little sauce at a time, push through a food mill to remove the tomato skins and seeds.

5 Place a few fresh basil leaves in each bottle and ladle in the sauce, filling to 2–3 cm from the top. Screw the lids on tightly.

6 Place a folded cloth or sheet of newspaper in the bottom of a pot. Sit the jars of sauce upright on top of the cloth or paper. Arrange another cloth or more sheets of newspaper between the jars to stop them knocking together as they boil.

7 Fill the pot with cold water and bring to the boil. Lower the heat and simmer for 2 hours. Check every now and then, and top up with more boiling water if necessary.

8 Turn the heat off and leave the jars to cool in the water. When cool, lift the jars out of the water, dry, and store in a cool, dark place for up to 12 months. Once opened, store in the refrigerator and use within 1 week.

Makes 2.25 litres

Autumn

Mushrooms

MUSHROOM AND THYME SOUP

A soup for mushroom lovers! This is the perfect soup for autumn, when mushrooms are abundant. It doesn't matter which variety you use, as long as they are the freshest you can find. I often combine mild varieties such as buttons with strongly flavoured varieties such as fields, swiss browns or shitaki. I also like to vary the texture of the soup, so sometimes I slice the mushrooms, and other times I finely chop them in a food processor.

Blitz the mushrooms in a food processor until they are finely chopped.

Melt the butter in a large heavy-based saucepan. Add the onion, garlic and bay leaf and fry gently for 3–4 minutes, until the onion is soft but not coloured. Add the mushrooms and thyme and cook gently for 3–4 minutes, until the mushrooms have softened. Increase the heat and add the stock. Bring to a boil, then lower the heat and simmer, covered, for 30 minutes.

Season to taste. Ladle into bowls and serve with big blobs of sour cream and a sprinkling of chives.

Serves 6–8

750 g mushrooms, wiped to remove any dirt, roughly chopped

100 g butter

1 medium onion, finely sliced

2 garlic cloves, crushed

1 bay leaf

3 tablespoons chopped thyme

2 litres chicken stock

salt

freshly ground black pepper

sour cream

3 tablespoons snipped chives

MUSHROOMS BAKED WITH A GARLICKY, HERBY CRUST

Large, flat field mushrooms are firm, satisfying and almost meaty. Baked with a crunchy topping, they make a perfect light lunch or starter. You'll only need a few lightly dressed salad leaves to accompany them, and perhaps some warm crusty bread. Add some fried chopped bacon to the topping if you like, or keep it vegetarian.

Preheat the oven to 180°C. Remove the stalks from 4 of the mushrooms, then finely chop the stalks with the remaining 2 mushrooms.

Melt the butter in a heavy-based saucepan. Add the onion and garlic and fry gently for 3–4 minutes, until the onion is soft but not coloured. Add the chopped mushrooms and stir well over the heat for a few minutes.

Remove from the heat and stir in the breadcrumbs, parsley, thyme and paprika and season with salt and pepper.

Arrange the 4 whole mushrooms on a baking tray. Brush them with the oil and season lightly. Mound the topping onto the mushrooms, then sprinkle on the parmesan. Bake for 20 minutes, or until the mushrooms are soft and the topping is golden and crunchy. Serve straight away with a crisp green salad.

Serves 4

6 large field mushrooms, wiped to remove any dirt

150 g butter

1 medium onion, finely chopped

4 garlic cloves, crushed

1½ cups breadcrumbs

3 tablespoons roughly chopped flat-leaf parsley

3 tablespoons chopped thyme

1 teaspoon sweet paprika

salt

freshly ground black pepper

3 tablespoons extra-virgin olive oil

20 g parmesan, grated

MIXED MUSHROOM RISOTTO WITH TRUFFLED PECORINO

To make a good risotto, you need to start with good stock, and this risotto begins by making a mushroom stock. This is combined with good-quality chicken stock which really intensifies the mushroom flavour. I love to serve this risotto with truffled pecorino instead of the more usual parmesan, as it adds another layer of pungent and rather mysterious earthy flavour.

To make the stock, combine the ingredients in a saucepan and bring to a simmer. Cook for 30–40 minutes, until the mushrooms have softened and released their liquid. Strain and reserve the mushrooms and stock separately.

To make the risotto, measure the volume of mushroom stock (there should be 400–500 ml) and add enough chicken stock to make up 1.5 litres. Pour into a saucepan and bring to a simmer.

Meanwhile, heat the oil in a large heavy-based saucepan. Add the onion, garlic and bay leaf and fry gently for 3–4 minutes, until the onion is soft but not coloured. Add the rice and cook gently, stirring, for 3–4 minutes.

Increase the heat and add the wine. Allow it to boil vigorously until most evaporates, then add the reserved mushrooms. Cook for 2–3 minutes, stirring, then add around half of the simmering stock. Cook for around 10 minutes, stirring frequently, until most of the stock has been absorbed.

Stir in the peas, then add the remaining stock a ladleful at a time, allowing each ladle to be absorbed before you add the next. Keep adding stock until the rice is cooked al dente — you may not need the full amount of stock.

Remove from the heat and stir in the parsley, thyme, butter and pecorino. Season with salt and pepper and stir well. Cover the pan and allow the risotto to rest for a minute before serving.

Serves 4

1–1.25 litres good-quality chicken stock

3 tablespoons olive oil

1 medium onion, finely diced

3 garlic cloves, crushed

1 bay leaf

300 g arborio rice

3 tablespoons white wine

60 g fresh peas (or frozen)

3 tablespoons roughly chopped flat-leaf parsley

2 tablespoons roughly chopped thyme

50 g butter

50 g truffled pecorino, grated

salt

freshly ground black pepper

Stock

100 g butter

500 g wild and cultivated mushrooms, wiped to remove any dirt, quartered

5 thyme sprigs

1 garlic clove, crushed

375 ml water

salt

freshly ground black pepper

Pickles

PICKLED BABY CUCUMBERS

Tiny pickled cucumbers — called cornichons — go brilliantly on charcuterie platters as their tangy crunch cuts through the richness of the cured meats. The addition of chilli makes these cucumbers a little spicy, just the way I like them.

They are really easy to make as once the jars are sterilised, you don't even have to do any cooking. You just put the cucumbers and aromatics in the jars and pour the vinegar on top, then seal and leave to pickle for a few weeks. If you can't find pickling cucumbers, lebanese cucumbers are just as good, although they do take longer to pickle. (To speed up the process, you can cut the cucumbers into 2 centimetre chunks, mix them with 100 grams of rock salt, and leave to stand for four hours before rinsing off the salt, patting dry and packing into jars.)

Pack the cucumbers into large sterilised jars with some of the onion, chilli, peppercorns, thyme and a bay leaf in each jar.

Stir the sugar and salt into the vinegar until dissolved, then pour into the jars to cover the cucumbers. Seal and store in a cool, dark place for 2–3 weeks before using. The cucumbers will keep for at least 3–6 months.

Makes 2 kg

2 kg baby pickling cucumbers, washed and thoroughly dried

1 large onion, finely sliced

3 small red chillies, halved lengthwise and seeded

2 tablespoons black peppercorns

10 thyme sprigs

bay leaves

75 g sugar

1 tablespoon salt

2 litres white wine vinegar

PICKLED BABY ONIONS

This is a quick and easy way to pickle onions, and you can vary the flavourings as you like. They are brilliant on an antipasto platter, or sliced and stuffed into a big cheese sandwich, or just to munch on with a cold beer.

Pack the onions into sterilised jars, dividing the chillies, garlic, bay leaves and rosemary evenly.

Combine the vinegar, sugar, cloves and peppercorns in a large, heavy-based saucepan or casserole and bring to a boil slowly, stirring gently until the sugar has all dissolved. Lower the heat and simmer for 2–3 minutes, then pour over the onions to cover.

Seal tightly and store in a cool dark place for 4 weeks before using. The pickled onions will keep for 3–6 months.

Makes 2 kg

2 kg small pickling onions, peeled
2 small red chilies, halved lengthwise
2 cloves garlic, sliced
2 bay leaves
1 sprig rosemary
2 litres white wine vinegar
400 g brown sugar
2 cloves
1 tablespoon black peppercorns

GIARDINIERA — ITALIAN PICKLED VEGETABLES

Many Italian kitchens boast jars of these brightly coloured pickles. They make a wonderful addition to any antipasto platter with cured meats and salamis and good crusty bread.

Mix the vegetables together and pack into large sterilised jars, adding some chilli, garlic, a little rosemary and a bay leaf to each jar.

Combine the vinegar, sugar, cloves and peppercorns in a saucepan and heat gently, stirring until the sugar dissolves. Increase the heat and bring to a simmer for 2–3 minutes, then remove from the heat and pour over the vegetables to cover.

Seal the jars and store in a cool, dark place for 4 weeks before using. The vegetables will keep for at least 3–6 months.

Makes 2 kg

500 g cauliflower, cut into small florets

500 g small pickling onions, peeled and cut into small pieces

500 g red capsicum, cut into small pieces

500 g carrots, cut into small pieces

2 small red chillies, halved lengthwise and seeded

2 garlic cloves, sliced

rosemary sprig

bay leaves

2 litres white wine vinegar

400 g brown sugar

2 cloves

1 tablespoon black peppercorns

PICKLED QUINCES

Here is a recipe for quinces in a sweet and spicy pickling liquid. You can use the liquid for all sorts of other fruits. However, different fruits need slightly different methods of preparation: hard fruits like quinces need to be simmered for about twenty minutes in the pickling liquid, while soft stone fruits such as peaches or plums don't need to be cooked, just immersed in the hot liquid and allowed to cool before bottling. (Also, stone fruits don't need to pickle as long and are ready to eat after two days.)

Serve pickled fruit on a cheese board, or with cured or smoked meats or fish. Chopped into small chunks, it also adds a fruity piquancy to salads.

Combine the pickling liquid ingredients in a pot and heat gently, stirring until the sugar dissolves. Increase the heat and bring to a boil. Add the quinces, lower the heat and simmer for 15–20 minutes, or until just soft (you don't want them to overcook and become mushy). Remove from the heat and allow the quinces to cool in the pickling liquid. Spoon into sterilised jars, dividing the aromatics evenly between the jars, then pour in enough liquid to cover the quinces. Seal and store in a cool, dark place for at least 1 week before using. The quinces will keep for 3–6 months.

Makes around 1.5 kg

6–8 quinces, peeled, quartered and cored

Pickling Liquid
1.2 litres white wine vinegar

500 ml water

770 g sugar

4 garlic cloves, sliced

5 bay leaves

2 teaspoons cloves

2 teaspoons black peppercorns

1 teaspoon allspice berries

Preserves

AUNTY RINA'S PRESERVED EGGPLANT

My lovely Italian godmother, Aunty Rina, taught me this method for preserving eggplant, and I always have a few jars in my pantry as it's so handy. I love serving a few slices on an antipasto platter, or stuffing some into a sandwich with the leftovers of a Sunday roast.

After pickling, you remove the eggplant slices as required, squeezing out as much vinegar as possible. You can drizzle them with extra-virgin olive oil and scatter on some chopped parsley. (If desired, squeeze the vinegar out from all of the slices at once and re-store them in olive oil.)

Layer the eggplant slices in a tray, scattering with the salt as you go. Cover with plastic wrap and weight with a chopping board. Put the tray in the refrigerator overnight to extract as much liquid from the eggplant as possible.

Rinse the eggplant in cold water and pat dry with paper towel. Pack into sterilised jars, putting a piece of chilli, some thyme and a bay leaf in each jar. Pour on the vinegar, seal and store in a cool, dark place for at least 4 weeks before using. The eggplant will keep for at least 3–6 months.

Makes around 1.5 kg

4 large eggplants, peeled and cut into 2 mm slices using a mandolin or a very sharp knife

80 g salt

1–2 small red chillies, halved lengthwise and seeded

5 thyme sprigs

bay leaves

1.5 litres white wine vinegar

PRESERVED PEARS WITH SAFFRON AND CARDAMOM

I always feel that pears are rather undervalued. They are a fantastic fruit that sees us happily through autumn and winter, and they come into their own when poached and served with breakfast muesli or with whipped cream and toasted almonds for an easy dessert. For something a touch more exotic, I poach them in a light sugar stock flavoured with saffron and cardamom, then store them in this liquid. Once you have opened the jar, the liquid can be reduced to a thick, golden syrup to drizzle over the pears when you serve them, or it can be re-used to poach more pears (although you might want to add a few fresh spices).

Beurre bosc pears are ideal for this recipe as they are firm and hold their shape well. Cut them in half or poach them whole, which always looks impressive.

Combine the water, sugar, cardamom, saffron and peppercorns in a pot. Heat gently, stirring until the sugar dissolves. Increase the heat and bring to a simmer for 2–3 minutes. Carefully add the pears and cover with a circle of baking paper (a cartouche) and a small plate to weight the pears down. Return to a simmer for 5 minutes, then remove from the heat. Spoon into a large jar or airtight container and cover with the hot poaching syrup. Seal and allow to cool, then store in the refrigerator for up to 3 months.

Makes around 1.2 kg

2 litres water

200 g sugar

2 tablespoons cardamom pods

1 teaspoon saffron threads, lightly crushed

2 black peppercorns

6 beurre bosc pears, peeled, halved and cored

MARINATED FETA WITH THYME, SAGE AND GARLIC

There are many types of feta, from firm, salty Greek feta to milder Bulgarian types, and my favourite — soft, creamy Danish feta.

All feta is stored and transported in brine, which keeps it from spoiling. I think the flavour is improved immeasurably by marinating it in olive oil for a few weeks. Some delicatessens sell expensive jars of this sort of feta, but it's far cheaper to marinate it yourself at home — and you have the fun of experimenting with different aromatics. This is an easy recipe to get you started. There are endless uses for this marinated feta. I like to crumble it into salads or over pastas and pizzas; I spread it onto crusty bread or add it to an antipasto platter.

Place the feta in jars. Add the aromatics and pour on enough olive oil to cover. Seal the jar and store in the refrigerator for 2 weeks before using. Once opened, use the feta within 2 weeks.

Makes 500 g

500 g Danish feta, cut in 3 cm cubes
$\frac{1}{4}$ cup thyme sprigs
$\frac{1}{4}$ cup sage leaves
3 garlic cloves, sliced into quarters
1 teaspoon black peppercorns
good-quality pure olive oil

MARINATED OLIVES WITH CHILLI AND FENNEL SEEDS

Most olives purchased from a delicatessen are preserved in brine, or in poor-quality olive oil. I much prefer to marinate them myself as I can use quality ingredients for a much better flavour.

Choose either black or green olives and rinse off the brine thoroughly before packing them into jars with the aromatics and oil. The oil can be re-used several times, so you can experiment with different olives each time. My favourites are tiny Ligurian olives; big, meaty green olives; and jumbo kalamata olives. Whichever olive you go for, my number-one rule when choosing them is to taste before you buy.

Pack the olives into jars, dividing the fennel seeds, chillies, peppercorns and bay leaves among them. Pour on enough olive oil to cover. Seal and store in a cool, dark place for 4 weeks before using. The olives will keep for at least 3–6 months.

Serve the olives as they are, or warm them gently in a frying pan to bring out the flavour and serve with a little chopped flat-leaf parsley.

Makes 1 kg

1 kg olives in brine, well rinsed and drained in a colander for 1 hour

25 g fennel seeds, lightly toasted

4 long red chillies, halved lengthwise

1 tablespoon black peppercorns

4 bay leaves

good-quality pure olive oil

chopped flat-leaf parsley to serve

Chutneys & RELISHES

APPLE, CURRANT AND CINNAMON RELISH

I serve this fruity relish with cold meats, and love to dollop it onto a chunk of farmhouse cheddar in a big doorstop sandwich.

Heat the oil in a large heavy-based saucepan. Add the onion and fry gently for 3–4 minutes, until soft but not coloured. Add the currants and fry for another 3 minutes. Add the apple and cook, stirring, for 2 minutes. Stir in the remaining ingredients and bring to a boil, then lower the heat and simmer for 30–40 minutes, stirring regularly. At the end of the cooking time, the relish should be reduced and thick. Taste and adjust the seasoning.

Spoon into sterilised jars, seal and leave to cool, then store in the refrigerator for 2 weeks before serving. Once opened, the relish will keep for 1 month.

Makes 1 litre

3 tablespoons olive oil

1 large onion, finely diced

160 g currants

1.5 kg granny smith apples, peeled, cored and cut into 1 cm dice

1 tablespoon ground cinnamon

1 tablespoon salt

1 teaspoon freshly ground white pepper

1 teaspoon dried mint

2 cloves

80 g brown sugar

250 ml apple cider vinegar

250 ml water

BEETROOT RELISH

Sweet and tangy, this vividly coloured relish livens up any meal. It's brilliant with roasts, a grilled steak or leftover cold meats, and I also think it's particularly good with smoked fish.

Place the beetroots in a large saucepan and cover with water. Add the white sugar and half the vinegar and heat gently until the sugar dissolves. Bring to a boil, then lower the heat and simmer for 1–2 hours, until the beetroots are tender. Allow to cool, then peel and cut into 1 cm dice.

Heat the oil in a large heavy-based saucepan. Add the onion and fry gently for 3–4 minutes, until soft but not coloured. Add the currants and ginger and fry for another 3 minutes. Add the diced beetroot along with the rest of the vinegar and remaining ingredients except the coriander. Bring to a boil, then lower the heat and simmer for 20 minutes, stirring regularly. At the end of the cooking time, the relish should be reduced and thick. Taste and adjust the salt, and leave to cool.

Once the relish has cooled, stir in the coriander and spoon into sterilised jars. Seal and store in the refrigerator for 2 weeks before serving. Once opened, the relish will keep for 1 month.

Makes 1 litre

2 large beetroots (about 1 kg)

2½ tablespoons white sugar

500 ml apple cider vinegar

3 tablespoons olive oil

1 large onion, finely diced

40 g currants

1 tablespoon grated ginger

2 granny smith apples, peeled and grated (to yield about 300 g)

3 cloves

1 teaspoon ground allspice

80 g brown sugar

½ tablespoon salt

250 ml water

salt

3 tablespoons **chopped coriander leaves**

INDIAN-SPICED TOMATO CHUTNEY

Chutneys are easy to make, and they're a great way of preserving fruits and vegetables from the end-of-summer glut. This recipe is one of my favourites; it has a hint of curry spice.

Heat the oil in a large heavy-based saucepan. Add the onion and garlic and fry gently for 3–4 minutes, until the onion is soft but not coloured. Add the ginger and fry for another minute. Stir in the spices and fry for 3–4 minutes, until the mixture is lovely and aromatic. Add the tomatoes and cook, stirring, for about 5 minutes. Stir in the sugar, vinegar and water and bring to a boil, then lower the heat and simmer for 1 hour, stirring regularly.

At the end of the cooking time, the chutney should be reduced and thick. Stir in the coriander and taste and adjust the salt.

Spoon into sterilised jars, seal and leave to cool, then store in the refrigerator for 2 weeks before serving. The chutney will keep in the fridge for up to 1 month.

Makes 1 litre

3 tablespoons olive oil

1 large onion, finely diced

4 garlic cloves, crushed

1 tablespoon grated ginger

1 teaspoon ground cumin, toasted

1 teaspoon ground coriander, toasted

1 teaspoon fenugreek seeds

1 tablespoon sweet paprika

1 teaspoon cayenne pepper

1 teaspoon freshly ground white pepper

$\frac{1}{2}$ tablespoon salt

1.5 kg roma tomatoes, roughly chopped

2 tablespoons raw sugar

$2\frac{1}{2}$ tablespoons white wine vinegar

500 ml water

1 cup roughly chopped coriander leaves

TOMATO RELISH

A really terrific all-purpose relish. I wouldn't eat a pie or sausage roll without it!

Whiz the tomatoes in a food processor to a coarse puree. Push through a food mill or strainer to remove the skins and seeds.

Heat the oil in a large heavy-based saucepan. Add the onion and garlic and fry gently for 4–5 minutes, until just beginning to colour. Add the tomato puree and bring to a boil, then add the remaining ingredients, return to the boil and reduce the heat to a simmer. Cook for 30 minutes, stirring frequently. At the end of the cooking time, the relish should be reduced and thick.

Spoon into sterilised jars, seal and leave to cool, then store in the refrigerator for up to 1 month.

Makes 700 ml

1 kg roma tomatoes, roughly chopped

3 tablespoons olive oil

1 medium onion, finely diced

3 garlic cloves, crushed

2 small red chillies, finely sliced (remove the seeds if you don't like too much heat)

150 g brown sugar

100 ml red wine vinegar

1 tablespoon worcestershire sauce

1 tablespoon salt

Soups

BORLOTTI BEAN SOUP

WHITE BEAN AND SAUSAGE SOUP

PORK AND PRAWN DUMPLINGS IN CHICKEN BROTH

LAMB SHANK AND BARLEY SOUP

SWEETCORN CHOWDER

THAI PUMPKIN SOUP

GARLICKY POTATO AND SPINACH SOUP

BORLOTTI BEAN SOUP

My nonna used to make this soup for my brother and me when we were small boys. In Italian it's called *pasta e fagioli*, and it's the best kind of country home-cooking there is. Nonna was quite thrifty, like many of her generation, so she would save up and freeze offcuts of fresh pasta that she made during the week and add them to her soup.

The soup is a complete meal, and a bit of a carbohydrate overload as it's full of beans, potatoes and pasta. Use fresh borlotti beans, which are in season during autumn. If you're smart, like my nonna, you'll pod them and freeze them to use at other times of the year, as this soup is fantastic in winter too. Otherwise, rinsed tinned beans or soaked and cooked dried beans will do.

Melt the butter in a large heavy-based saucepan. Add the onion, garlic and bay leaf and fry gently for 3–4 minutes, until the onion is soft but not coloured. Add the beans and potato, followed by the stock. Bring to a boil, skimming away any foam or impurities that rise to the surface. Lower the heat and simmer, uncovered, for 30 minutes, or until the beans and potato are both tender.

Remove the potato and mash it in a small bowl with a few tablespoons of hot soup. Stir back into the soup to thicken it. Season to taste with salt and pepper. Add the pasta and simmer for another 2–3 minutes or until cooked. Serve scattered with the parsley and parmesan and with a drizzle of extra-virgin olive oil.

Serves 4–6

100 g butter

1 large onion, finely diced

2 garlic cloves, crushed

1 bay leaf

2 kg fresh borlotti beans, podded to yield 1 kg

2 large potatoes, peeled and quartered

2 litres chicken stock

salt

freshly ground black pepper

200 g fresh pasta, or cooked dried pasta (preferably a small variety)

$\frac{1}{2}$ cup roughly chopped flat-leaf parsley

30 g parmesan, grated

extra-virgin olive oil

WHITE BEAN AND SAUSAGE SOUP

This is one of those dishes that is a little different each time I make it. Sometimes I'll use chorizo or salami, sometimes leftover cooked Italian sausages, sometimes fresh sausages. I'll usually vary the vegetables depending on what's in my fridge. One ingredient that remains a constant, though, is a hunk of smoked bacon, rather than the usual rashers of cured bacon. Ask at a deli for an end piece (tell them you're making soup). It may not look pretty, but it will add loads of flavour.

Drain the beans and place them in a saucepan with plenty of fresh cold water. Bring to a boil, then remove from the heat and set aside.

Heat the butter and oil in a large saucepan. Add the onion, garlic and bacon and fry gently for 3–4 minutes, until the onion is soft but not coloured.

Stir in the sausage pieces (don't worry if they disintegrate) followed by the carrot, celery and bay leaf. Pour in the wine and stock and bring to a boil. Lower the heat and simmer for 5 minutes.

Drain the beans and add to the soup with the cabbage and fennel. Return to a boil, then lower the heat and simmer, uncovered, for 30–40 minutes, or until the beans are soft.

Season to taste with salt and pepper. Scatter on the parsley and serve with warm crusty bread.

Serves 6–8

450 g haricot beans, soaked overnight

50 g butter

2 tablespoons olive oil

2 onions, finely diced

2 garlic cloves, crushed

200 g piece of smoked bacon, roughly chopped

400 g fresh Italian-style sausages, cut into 2 cm slices

2 carrots, diced

2 celery stalks, diced

1 bay leaf

200 ml white wine

2 litres chicken stock

$\frac{1}{4}$ savoy cabbage, cut into 2 cm squares

$\frac{1}{2}$ fennel bulb, cut into 2 cm squares

salt

freshly ground black pepper

1 cup roughly chopped flat-leaf parsley

PORK AND PRAWN DUMPLINGS IN CHICKEN BROTH

Chinese dumplings aren't hard to make, and good-quality wrappers are readily available in Asian supermarkets. I like to make dumpling soup at home with my boys as it's a fun kitchen activity that we can all do together in a sort of mini production line. Make sure the pork and prawn meat for the dumpling filling is well chilled.

To make the broth, combine all the ingredients in a pot. Slowly bring to a boil, skimming away any foam or impurities that rise to the surface. Lower the heat and simmer very gently, uncovered, for 2 hours. Skim regularly and top up with cold water if necessary. Remove from the heat and cool briefly, then ladle through a sieve. Chill in the refrigerator, then skim off any surface fat. From this stage you can proceed straight away to make the soup (you will need 1 litre of stock), or divide it into batches and refrigerate or freeze for future use.

To make the dumplings, combine all the ingredients except the wrappers in a food processor and pulse for 10–20 seconds to a smooth, fine consistency.

Lay a wrapper out on a work surface and place a teaspoon of filling in the centre. Lightly brush the edges with water and fold the wrapper in half. Press the edges firmly to seal. Now bring the ends together around your index finger and overlap them, forming a ring. Moisten the ends and press them together to seal. Continue making dumplings with the remaining wrappers and filling. Cover with a tea towel and refrigerate if not using straight away.

To make a dipping sauce, mix the soy sauce, vinegar, chilli and sugar in a bowl. Put the spring onions and shallots in separate small bowls.

Reheat the broth and season to taste. Bring another large saucepan of water to a boil, then lower to a healthy simmer. Add the dumplings in batches and cook for 3–5 minutes. Remove with a slotted spoon and drain on a tea towel while you cook the rest.

Divide the dumplings between serving bowls and ladle on the hot broth. Serve with the dipping sauce, spring onions and shallots on the side.

Serves 4

200 g finely minced pork

100 g prawn meat, finely chopped

2 tablespoons finely snipped chives

2 tablespoons finely sliced coriander leaves

½ teaspoon crushed garlic

1 teaspoon finely grated ginger

1 tablespoon soy sauce

¼ teaspoon sesame oil

1 packet round dumpling wrappers

Broth

1 kg chicken bones

2–3 litres water

125 ml soy sauce

3 tablespoons kecap manis (Indonesian sweet soy sauce)

1 large carrot, chopped

1 celery stalk, chopped

1 large onion, chopped

3 garlic cloves, peeled

4 cm piece of ginger, sliced

3 thyme sprigs

1 bay leaf

1 teaspoon black peppercorns

¼ cup coriander roots, cleaned

To Serve

3 tablespoons soy sauce

2 tablespoons rice vinegar

½ long red chilli, sliced

1 teaspoon sugar

3 spring onions, finely sliced

3 tablespoons deep-fried shallots

LAMB SHANK AND BARLEY SOUP

The secret to this soup lies in using a really rich and deeply flavoured homemade lamb stock. Sometimes I want the stock to be extra tasty and I use a base of chicken stock, but water will also do the job.

To make the stock, put the lamb neck and shanks in a pot. Pour on the chicken stock or water and bring to a simmer. Skim away any foam or impurities that rise to the surface, then add the remaining ingredients. Top up with more water and return to a simmer. Cook gently for $2\frac{1}{2}$–3 hours. Remove the shanks from the pan, pull the meat from the bones and refrigerate until ready to use. Strain the stock through a sieve. Chill in the refrigerator, then skim off any surface fat.

When ready to make the soup, melt the butter in a large heavy-based saucepan. Add the onion and garlic and fry gently for 3–4 minutes, until the onion is soft but not coloured. Add the drained barley, fennel and stock. Bring to a boil, then lower the heat and simmer for $1\frac{1}{2}$ hours, until the barley is soft.

Add the lamb meat together with the herbs. Season to taste and serve with a big squeeze of lemon.

Serves 6–8

2 tablespoons butter

2 onions, finely diced

4 garlic cloves, crushed

200 g pearl barley, soaked overnight

2 large fennel bulbs, finely sliced

3 tablespoons chopped dill

1 tablespoon chopped thyme

salt

freshly ground black pepper

juice of 1 lemon

Stock

1 lamb neck

2 lamb shanks

2 litres chicken stock or water

2 large onions, roughly chopped

4 garlic cloves, peeled

3 carrots, roughly chopped

2 celery stalks, roughly chopped

2 bay leaves

1 tablespoon fennel seeds

1 teaspoon black peppercorns

1 teaspoon salt

SWEETCORN CHOWDER

I find that sweetcorn grows like weeds in my garden, so I like to have lots of recipes up my sleeve for when the kids are tired of corn on the cob. They adore this creamy, thick soup, full of juicy corn kernels and little salty pieces of fried bacon. Don't worry if you are not a gardener — corn is as cheap as chips when it's in season.

If you want to keep this soup vegetarian, omit the bacon and use vegetable stock. The quickest way to knock up some quick vegie stock is to boil the cobs of corn first, then slice off the kernels to add to the soup towards the end of the cooking time. Use the cooking water as instant stock.

Melt the butter in a large heavy-based saucepan. Add the onion and fry gently for 3–4 minutes, until soft but not coloured. Add the bacon and fry until lightly browned. Add the corn kernels and potato, followed by the stock, and bring to a boil. Lower the heat and simmer for 15–20 minutes, until the corn and potato are both tender.

Puree the soup, then taste and season it to your liking. Stir in the cream and serve garnished with the chives.

Serves 6–8

100 g butter

1 onion, finely diced

100 g thick-cut bacon, finely diced

10 cobs of sweetcorn, kernels sliced off

2 large potatoes, peeled and cut into 1 cm dice

2 litres chicken or vegetable stock

salt

freshly ground black pepper

100 ml cream

3 tablespoons finely snipped chives

THAI PUMPKIN SOUP

Asian flavours really seem to enhance the sweetness of pumpkin, and they liven up this familiar Aussie favourite. You can make it with a good-quality commercial curry paste, but the flavours are much fresher if you whiz up your own.

To make the paste, combine the ingredients in a food processor and whiz to a paste, adding a little water if needed to bring it all together.

Heat the oil in a large heavy-based saucepan. Add the paste and fry gently for 3–4 minutes until fragrant. Add the pumpkin, carrot and water and bring to a boil. Lower the heat and simmer for 5 minutes, then add the palm sugar, fish sauce, lime leaf and coconut milk. Simmer for 20 minutes, until the pumpkin is very tender.

Puree the soup, then taste and season it to your liking. Stir in the lime juice and serve garnished with coriander, spring onions and shreds of chilli.

Serves 6–8

2 tablespoons vegetable oil

1 kg pumpkin, skinned, seeded and diced

1 carrot, finely diced

2 litres water

25 g palm sugar

1 tablespoon fish sauce

1 kaffir lime leaf

400 ml coconut milk

salt

freshly ground black pepper

juice of 3 limes

½ cup roughly chopped coriander leaves

2 spring onions, finely sliced

1 long red chilli, sliced into fine shreds

Curry Paste

1 onion, roughly chopped

2 garlic cloves, crushed

50 g ginger, peeled and roughly chopped

½ lemongrass stalk (split it lengthwise), bruised with the back of a knife, roughly chopped

1 small red chilli, seeded and roughly chopped

2 cups coriander roots and stalks, cleaned and roughly chopped

GARLICKY POTATO AND SPINACH SOUP

Potato and spinach are a match made in heaven, especially when combined with loads of garlic. Don't be frightened by the amount in this recipe — it cooks to a lovely mild sweetness, especially if you can find young, fresh, tender garlic (or grow your own).

Melt the butter in a large heavy-based saucepan. Add the garlic, onion, leek, celery, bay leaf and thyme and fry gently for 3–4 minutes, until soft but not coloured. Add the stock and bring to a boil. Lower the heat and simmer, uncovered, for 45 minutes.

Add the potato and cook for a further 15 minutes, until soft. Throw in the spinach and cook briefly until it wilts. Season to taste, then stir in the lemon juice. Scatter on the parsley and serve.

Serves 6

75 g butter

3 heads of garlic, cloves peeled and crushed

1 large onion, finely diced

2 leeks, finely sliced

2 celery stalks, finely sliced

1 bay leaf

1 tablespoon chopped thyme

1.5 litres chicken stock

4 potatoes, peeled and cut into 1.5 cm slices

300 g baby spinach leaves, roughly chopped

salt

freshly ground black pepper

juice of 1 lemon

$\frac{1}{2}$ cup roughly chopped flat-leaf parsley

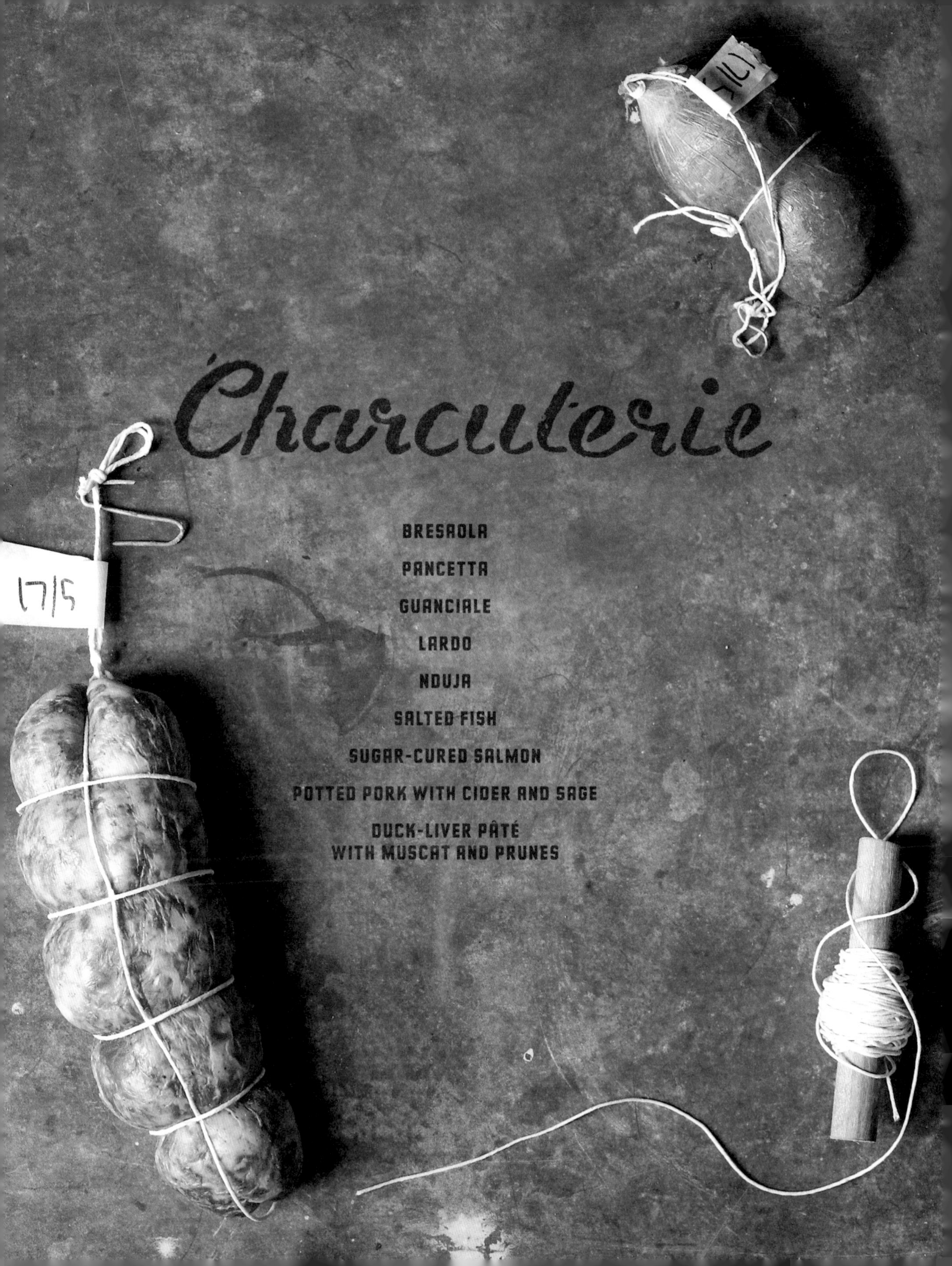

Charcuterie

BRESAOLA

PANCETTA

GUANCIALE

LARDO

NDUJA

SALTED FISH

SUGAR-CURED SALMON

POTTED PORK WITH CIDER AND SAGE

DUCK-LIVER PÂTÉ
WITH MUSCAT AND PRUNES

CHARCUTERIE IS just a fancy name for smallgoods or preserved meat products. It includes things like sausages and bacon, the endless array of salamis and hams, and also pâtés, terrines and confits.

A lot of these items come from Europe, and they evolved from the days when families needed to find ways of preserving meat to eat in the cold winter months. In the village in northern Italy where my grandfather grew up, the pig butcher would come around every autumn to dispatch the family's specially reared pig, then the whole animal would be processed from the nose down to the tail.

Although there isn't the same need to provide food for winter these days, it's a tradition that is still carried on in many European families. In my family, it's Uncle Aldo and Uncle Guido who hand out homemade salamis and prosciuttos — and they are delicious! I think it's brilliant that these techniques are being kept alive.

Most of the small, artisanal producers of smallgoods have been forced out of the market by stringent health and safety regulations. Disappointingly, the big manufacturers often take the easy way out, so most of the stuff you buy in shops is actually cooked meat rather than traditional fermented, cured or dried products. The problem is that the products lose their individuality and flavour.

Charcuterie is one of my real passions and you'd be amazed how easy it is to prepare at home. 'Garage salami', I call it! I've included a few of my favourite recipes here, and I encourage you to start with something fairly easy such as the salami on page 198. If you're like me, you'll be so excited by the results that before long you'll want to experiment with other preserving techniques too.

Masterclass

HOW TO MAKE SALAMI

juice of 1 lemon

2 bungs (these are large
natural sausage casings,
usually from pig, sheep or
cattle, that you can order
from your butcher) — but
buy extras in case of tears

2 kg pork neck, chilled

400 g pork back fat, chilled

salt flakes

1 tablespoon freshly ground
white pepper

3 tablespoons fennel seeds

3 tablespoons grappa

1 Fill a bowl with lukewarm water and stir in the lemon juice. Soak the sausage casings for 10–15 minutes.

2 With a very sharp knife, trim away any tendons, sinew or bits of bone from the pork neck and discard. Cut the meat into 2 cm dice.

3 Slice the skin away from the back fat and discard. Cut the fat into 2 cm dice.

4 Weigh the combined meat and fat. Calculate 2.8 per cent of the weight — which should be somewhere around 60 g — and weigh out that amount of salt. Combine the meat and fat, salt and pepper in a mixing bowl and mix well.

5 Push the mixture through a mincer fitted with a 6 mm plate, directly onto a work surface.

6 Scatter the fennel seeds and grappa onto the minced meat.

7 Use your hands to knead the mixture vigorously for 5–10 minutes, until it becomes nice and sticky.

8 Remove the sausage casings from the water and fill the ox bung carefully, packing the mixture in right down to the closed end, ensuring you don't trap any pockets of air that could cause the salamis to spoil from within.

CONTINUED »

9

10

11

9 Once all of the filling is used, tie the open end of the bung tightly with string.

10 Prick the salamis a few times with a sharp pin to expel any air pockets.

11 Hang the salamis in a cool, dry, well-ventilated place for 2–3 months (a garage is ideal). Over time, water will evaporate from the salami and it will become dry and hard. Natural white moulds may bloom on the outside surface, but these are not harmful and they add flavour.

12 Cut off slices as required. Once cut, store the salami in an airtight container and refrigerate. It will keep for up to 2 months.

Makes 2 x 20 cm salamis

BRESAOLA

Bresaola is a classic Italian air-dried meat, a bit like prosciutto or Spanish jamón. It's one of my very favourite smallgood items and it's really easy to make yourself at home.

The best cut for bresaola is beef girello, which has an intense meaty flavour. The girello is cured in a red-wine brine for a week, which turns the meat a gorgeous deep red. It is then hung in a cool, breezy spot to dry, such as a garage.

To make the brine, combine the ingredients in a non-reactive saucepan and heat gently until the salt has dissolved. Increase the heat and bring to a vigourous boil for 2 minutes. Remove from the heat and leave to cool overnight.

Trim the girello of any fat or sinew. Pour the brine into a deep container and immerse the girello, making sure it is completely submerged in brine. Place a plate and a weight on top to keep the girello submerged. Cover and refrigerate for 7 days, turning the girello over every day.

Remove the girello from the brine (discard the brine) and pat the meat dry. Pierce a sharp metal skewer through one end of the girello, twice, to form 2 holes. Thread a long length of strong butcher's string through both holes and hang the girello in a cool, dry, well-ventilated place for 4–6 weeks (a garage is ideal).

By the end of this time, much of the moisture will have evaporated from the meat. It will feel hard to touch and you may see a white mould forming on the surface, but this is a good mould that is not harmful and adds flavour. Once you cut the bresaola, store it in an airtight container in the refrigerator, where it will keep for up to 2 months.

To serve the bresaola, slice it as thinly as you can and arrange the slices overlapping on a large platter. Drizzle with extra-virgin olive oil and sprinkle with salt flakes.

Makes 1 kg

1.5 kg piece of beef girello

Red-wine Brine
1.25 litres red wine
500 ml water
150 g salt
1 tablespoon black peppercorns
1 tablespoon allspice berries
2 bay leaves

PANCETTA

Pancetta is cured pork belly, a kind of Italian bacon. It's sometimes left flat, and sometimes rolled into long logs. Like bacon, it's sometimes smoked as well. But whatever the finished shape and regardless of whether it's smoked or not, pancetta is always air-dried, which means you don't have to cook it. This is a quick and easy way of preparing it yourself at home.

You will have to order a large piece of pork belly from your butcher. Ask for a free-range or organic pig if possible, as they are reared more humanely and the flavour is far superior. Also ask your butcher to remove the skin and any bits of bone and cartilage.

Combine the ingredients for the curing salt in a mixing bowl. Spread a thick layer over the base of a plastic tray. Lay the pork belly onto the salt and rub more handfuls of salt all over it. Pack salt around the pork and leave in a cool place for 24 hours. (There should be leftover salt.)

After 24 hours, you'll see that some of the salt cure has liquified to form a pool beneath the belly. Drain the liquid away and rub more salt over the pork. Repeat this process daily for 4 more days, ensuring that all surfaces of the pork are always covered with salt.

At the end of the curing time, wipe the salt away with your hands. Rinse the pork with red wine.

Pierce a sharp metal skewer through the narrower end of the belly, twice, to form 2 holes. Combine the pepper rub ingredients in a small bowl and rub all over the pork, including into either side of the pierced holes. Thread a long length of strong butcher's string through both holes and hang the belly in a cool, dry, well-ventilated place for 6–8 weeks (a garage is ideal).

By the end of this time, the pancetta will be fairly dry and firm. To serve, slice the pancetta as finely as you can and serve it on its own or as part of a charcuterie platter. Once cut, store the pancetta in an airtight container in the refrigerator for up to 2 months.

Makes 2.5–3 kg

3–4 kg piece of pork belly
red wine

Spiced Curing Salt
4 kg rock salt
100 g freshly ground white pepper
50 g freshly ground black pepper
50 g dried chilli flakes
½ cup picked rosemary leaves
3 tablespoons ground allspice

Pepper Rub
100 g freshly ground white pepper
3 tablespoons dried oregano
1 tablespoon ground allspice

GUANCIALE

For me, guanciale is the king of Italian smallgoods. It is a speciality of central Italy and is traditionally used in authentic *spaghetti alla carbonara*. The name comes from *'guancia'*, the word for 'cheek', and it is a brilliant piece of meat — thick, soft and a bit fatty, with a really intense porky flavour. Guanciale is quite difficult to find outside Italy, but luckily it's easy to make at home. You'll need to ask your butcher for a pig's cheek in advance, and get him to trim away the glands for you.

Guanciale is not usually eaten raw (although it can be), but is usually sliced thinly and fried like bacon.

Combine the ingredients for the curing salt in a mixing bowl. Spread a thick layer over the base of a plastic tray. Lay the pig's cheek onto the salt and rub more handfuls of salt all over it. Pack the remaining salt around the cheek, completely covering it, and refrigerate for 3 weeks.

At the end of the curing time, wipe the salt away with your hands. Pierce a sharp metal skewer through one end of the cheek, twice, to form 2 holes. Combine the pepper and chilli rub ingredients in a small bowl and rub all over the cheek, including into either side of the pierced holes. Thread a long length of strong butcher's string through both holes and hang the cheek in a cool, dry, well-ventilated place for 5 weeks (a garage is ideal).

By the end of this time, the guanciale will have shrunk and become quite firm. Slice as required. Once cut, store in an airtight container in the refrigerator for up to 2–3 months.

Makes 750 g

1 kg pig's cheek (jowl), glands and skin removed

Spiced Curing Salt

2 kg rock salt

100 g fennel seeds, ground

50 g freshly ground white pepper

50 g freshly ground black pepper

3 tablespoons roughly chopped thyme

Pepper and Chilli Rub

3 tablespoons freshly ground white pepper

3 tablespoons dried chilli flakes

LARDO

Lardo is sometimes called white prosciutto or pork 'butter'. It's a thick piece of pork back fat, usually from a larger female pig, that is salt-cured for several months then rubbed with ground white pepper and air-dried for several more months.

Lardo has many uses in the Italian kitchen. It's primarily used wherever you need to add extra fat or flavour to an otherwise lean cut of meat — it's often cut into slices and draped over the meat before roasting (see Quail Baked with Lardo, Lemon and Vine Leaves, page 236) — and is even just added to a frying pan instead of a lump of butter. It's also slipped into braised pulses and soups to add flavour and sheen.

To be honest, I love lardo when it's cut into wafer-thin slices and squished onto crusty bread with salt and pepper and a drizzle of extra-virgin olive oil. This is how it's eaten in the rural areas of northern Italy during the chilly winters, when people need the extra calories to keep them going during a hard day's physical work.

Combine the ingredients for the curing salt in a mixing bowl. Spread a thick layer over the base of a plastic tray. Lay the piece of back fat onto the salt and rub more handfuls of salt all over it. Pack the remaining salt around the back fat, completely covering it, and refrigerate for 2 months. Reserve the remaining curing salt.

At the end of the curing time, remove the back fat from the salt and wipe off any remaining salt with your hands. Pierce a sharp metal skewer through one end of the back fat, twice, to form 2 holes. Rub the back fat all over with white pepper, including into either side of the pierced holes. Thread a long length of strong butcher's string through both holes and hang the back fat in a cool, dry, well-ventilated place for 8 weeks (a garage is ideal).

By the end of this time, the lardo will be quite dry and firm. Slice as required. Once cut, store in an airtight container in the refrigerator for up to 2–3 months.

Makes 1.8 kg

2 kg piece of pork back fat, skin removed

100 g freshly ground white pepper

Spiced Curing Salt

3 kg rock salt

100 g fennel seeds, ground

100 g freshly ground white pepper

30 g dried chilli flakes

1 cup roughly chopped rosemary leaves

NDUJA

Pronounced 'en-dool-ya', nduja is a red-hot spicy salami from Calabria. It's traditionally made from the pig's head minus the cheeks, which are used for Guanciale (page 205), and it gets a distinctive red colour from a paste of chilli, capsicum and tomato.

Traditionally, salamis are made using around three per cent salt to meat, but nduja uses only two per cent, which means you end up with a softer, almost spreadable sausage. Nduja is usually served on slices of bread or bruschetta or alongside ripe, strong cheese, but is also great cooked in pasta sauces or crumbled onto pizzas.

To make the chilli paste, combine the ingredients in a large heavy-based saucepan and bring to a boil. Lower the heat and simmer, uncovered, for 2 hours, stirring regularly. By the end you should have a thick paste. Puree in a food processor, then push through a food mill to remove any remaining skins. Allow to cool, then refrigerate until ready to use.

Fill a bowl with lukewarm water and stir in the lemon juice. Soak the sausage casings for 10–15 minutes.

Combine the minced fat and meat, salt, wine and spices in a mixing bowl. Measure out 500 ml of chilli paste and add to the bowl. Mix well, then transfer to a work surface and knead vigorously for 5–10 minutes, until nice and sticky.

Remove the sausage casings from the water. Fill the ox bung carefully, packing the mixture in right down to the closed end, ensuring that you don't trap any pockets of air which would cause the nduja to spoil from within. Tie the open end tightly with string and and prick a few times with a sharp skewer to expel any air pockets.

Hang the nduja in a cool, dry, well-ventilated place for 6 months (a garage is ideal). Over time, water will evaporate from the nduja, but it will remain quite soft.

Slice as required. Once cut, put in a jar (as the nduja is soft, you should be able to squeeze it in), cover with olive oil and store in the refrigerator. It will keep this way for up to 2 months.

Makes 2 x 20 cm salamis

juice of 1 lemon

2 ox bungs (large natural sausage casings) — but buy extras in case of tears

750 kg minced pork back fat (to mince it yourself, follow the directions on page 198)

1.75 kg minced pork neck (to mince it yourself, follow the directions on page 198)

50 g salt

3 tablespoons red wine

1 tablespoon sweet paprika

1 tablespoon fennel seeds, ground

Chilli Paste

1 kg small red chillies, seeded and chopped

500 g red capsicum, seeded and chopped

500 g tomatoes, seeded and chopped

1 garlic clove, crushed

500 ml water

SALTED FISH

Have you ever wondered about those large, stiff-as-a-board white fish that you see hanging in European delis? They are *baccala* — salt cod — and are greatly loved by Italians, Spanish and Portuguese.

Although salt cod is widely available, I like to salt my own local fish at home, and add aromatics to enhance the flavour. Salted fish has a unique flavour and makes fantastic soups and stews, and can be whipped with olive oil (and sometimes potatoes) to make brandade. I like to serve it with egg or rice dishes or flake it into salads to serve with thick slices of sourdough toast rubbed with garlic and extra-virgin olive oil.

Combine the ingredients for the curing salt in a mixing bowl. Spread a thick layer over the base of a plastic tray. Lay the piece of rockling onto the salt and rub more handfuls of salt all over it. Pack the remaining salt around the fish, completely covering it, and refrigerate for 2–3 months.

At the end of the curing time, remove the fish from the salt and rinse it well. It will be quite firm and stiff, as the salt will have drawn out the moisture. Pat it dry then wrap in plastic wrap and store in an airtight container in the fridge for up to 1 month.

Before using, the baccala needs to be soaked in cold water for at least 24 hours, changing the soaking water twice. Transfer it to a large, heavy-based saucepan and cover with fresh cold water. Bring to a simmer and cook for 20–30 minutes, until the fish is tender. Remove from the cooking water (you can leave it to cool in the water if convenient) and peel away the skin and remove any bones. Break into rough flakes and use as desired.

Makes 1 kg

1.5 kg side of rockling
(or use blue eye or another large, firm white fish), skin left on

Spiced Curing Salt

3 kg rock salt

2 cups roughly chopped dill

50 g fennel seeds

50 g freshly ground black pepper

1 teaspoon dried chilli flakes

SUGAR-CURED SALMON

This is a twist on the Swedish classic, gravlax. It is a really easy and impressive dish to serve when you're entertaining and it goes quite a long way.

Slice the salmon very thinly, arrange the slices over a large platter and serve with Lemon Thyme and Mustard Dressing (page 47) or Horseradish Cream (page 248), and with sourdough bread. Alternatively, arrange bite-sized pieces of salmon on top of blinis or tiny croutons and serve with pre-dinner drinks.

Combine the ingredients for the sugar cure in a mixing bowl.

Line a tray with 2 large pieces of plastic wrap and a piece of foil, allowing enough hanging over the edge to wrap up the salmon. Put a third of the cure mixture in the tray, covering the base evenly. Place the piece of salmon skin-side down on top, then cover with the remaining cure mixture, patting it on in a thick, even layer.

Wrap the fish tightly in the foil and seal well. Wrap tightly in the 2 layers of plastic wrap. Place a board and a weight on top of the fish and refrigerate for 24 hours, turning the parcel once.

Unwrap the fish and scrape off the cure mixture. Rinse the fish under cold water and pat dry with paper towel. Keep chilled in the refrigerator until ready to slice and serve.

Serves 12

1 kg side of salmon, pin bones removed, skin left on

Sugar Cure

150 g raw sugar

150 g caster sugar

300 g rock salt

3 tablespoons cumin seeds, toasted and ground

3 tablespoons coriander seeds, toasted and ground

grated zest of 2 oranges

Masterclass

HOW TO CURE FISH

1.4 kg side of kingfish, pin bones removed, skin left on

3 tablespoons vodka

3 tablespoons finely chopped dill

Curing Mixture

200 g rock salt

200 g raw sugar

$\frac{1}{2}$ cup roughly chopped thyme

$\frac{1}{2}$ cup roughly chopped flat-leaf parsley

$\frac{1}{2}$ cup roughly chopped dill

1 tablespoon freshly ground white pepper

grated zest of 1 orange

$1\frac{1}{2}$ tablespoons Grand Marnier

SERVING SUGGESTIONS

Slice thinly with dill and rye bread; through a salad with rocket and mustard dressing; or it's delicious just lightly seared.

NOTE

Here I cure kingfish, but you could just as easily cure salmon, trout, snapper or blue eye.

1 Combine the ingredients for the curing mixture in a bowl.

2 Line a tray with 2 large pieces of plastic wrap and a piece of foil, allowing enough hanging over the edge to wrap up the fish. Put a third of the curing mixture in the tray, covering the base evenly.

3 Place the piece of kingfish skin-side down on top, then cover with the remaining cure mixture, patting it on in a thick, even layer.

4 Wrap the fish tightly in the foil and seal well. Wrap tightly in the 2 layers of plastic wrap.

5 Place a board or tray and a weight on top of the fish and refrigerate for 24 hours, turning the parcel once.

6 Unwrap the fish and scrape off the curing mixture. Rinse the fish under cold water and pat dry with paper towel.

7 Splash the vodka over the fish and massage it in gently, then sprinkle on an even layer of dill. Refrigerate until ready to serve.

8 Carve the chilled kingfish into wafer-thin slices and serve with onion rings, capers, sour cream mixed with chives, and dark rye bread.

Serves 6–8

POTTED PORK WITH CIDER AND SAGE

Potted meats are considered a bit old-fashioned these days, but they are a lovely way of using the less-tender secondary cuts. Simmered gently with aromatics, the meat fibres soften and melt and the flavours intensify. You set the meat in an earthenware dish and serve it as a delicious spread, perhaps with crusty bread and Pickled Baby Cucumbers (page 166) or pickled onions.

Combine all the ingredients except the black pepper and parsley in a large heavy-based saucepan and bring to a boil. Skim away any foam or impurities that rise to the surface, then lower the heat and simmer for 20 minutes, stirring frequently. Cover the pan and cook on the lowest heat for 1 hour. Check the pan every now and then to make sure the meat is not sticking to the bottom. By the end of the cooking time, much of the liquid should have evaporated and the meat should be completely tender and submerged in fatty cooking juices.

Strain, reserving the juices. Remove the bay leaf and cinnamon stick from the meat and roughly crush the meat with a fork. Transfer to the bowl of an electric mixer fitted with a beater. Turn the motor on low and begin beating the meat as you slowly pour in the cooking juices (reserve a few tablespoons of juices). Continue beating for a minute or so.

Season the meat with a little extra salt and add the black pepper and parsley. Spoon into a 750 ml–1 litre earthenware dish, packing the meat in well, and smooth the surface. Pour on the reserved juices to cover the surface of the meat. Leave to cool, then cover with plastic wrap and store in the refrigerator for up to 7 days. The top layer of juices, which solidifies as a layer of fat, helps the meat to keep.

Serves 6–8

1 kg pork neck, cut into 1.5 cm dice

450 g pork back fat, cut into 1.5 cm dice

330 ml apple cider

250 ml water

2 tablespoons apple cider vinegar

small handful of sage leaves

1 bay leaf

3 cloves

1 cinnamon stick

2 teaspoons salt

$\frac{1}{2}$ teaspoon freshly ground white pepper

$\frac{1}{2}$ teaspoon freshly ground black pepper

$\frac{1}{2}$ cup finely chopped flat-leaf parsley

DUCK-LIVER PÂTÉ WITH MUSCAT AND PRUNES

Smooth pâtés always seem more sophisticated than rustic terrines and potted meats, and this recipe is definitely rather grown-up, with the addition of prunes, muscat and brandy. Serve it with triangles of thin, crisp toast with pre-dinner drinks, or as a smart dinner-party starter.

Combine the prunes, muscat and brandy in a bowl and leave to macerate overnight.

Tip the prunes and liquid into a food processor and blend to a smooth paste.

Heat the oil in a heavy-based frying pan and briefly fry the livers in batches, until golden brown on the outside but rare and soft in the middle. Transfer the warm livers to the food processor with the prunes and blend briefly. Add 300 g of the butter as well as the cream, salt, pepper and thyme and blend to a smooth puree.

Spoon into a 750 ml bowl (or several smaller bowls) and smooth the surface. Melt the remaining butter and pour it over the pâté to seal it. Leave to cool, then cover with plastic wrap and store in the refrigerator for up to 7 days. The layer of butter helps the pâté to keep.

Serves 6–8

100 g pitted prunes, roughly chopped

100 ml muscat

2 tablespoons brandy

2 tablespoons olive oil

900 g duck livers, trimmed of sinew and any greenish bits to yield around 800 g

400 g butter at room temperature

100 ml cream

2 teaspoons salt

1 teaspoon freshly ground white pepper

1 tablespoon chopped thyme

Masterclass

HOW TO MAKE TERRINE

10 long smoked bacon rashers,
rinds removed, to line the terrine,
plus 200 g thick slices cut into
1 cm dice

1½ tablespoons butter

1 small onion, finely diced

2 garlic cloves, crushed

1 teaspoon chopped thyme

1 teaspoon chopped sage leaves

¼ teaspoon ground allspice

1 kg pork neck or belly, trimmed
and finely minced

400 g free-range chicken breast,
cut into 2 cm dice

2 tablespoons dijon mustard

2 tablespoons sweet sherry

2 teaspoons salt

1 teaspoon freshly ground
black pepper

1 egg

NOTE
*You can make many different kinds
of terrines. This is a country-style
terrine.*

1 Preheat the oven to 160°C. Line a 1 litre terrine mould with plastic
wrap. Line the mould crosswise with the bacon rashers, leaving
enough overhang to bring them around the top of the terrine.

2 Heat the butter in a small frying pan. Add the onion, garlic,
thyme, sage and allspice and sweat gently for 3–4 minutes, until
the onion is soft but not coloured. Tip into a large mixing bowl
and leave to cool completely.

3 Add the remaining ingredients and use your hands to mix
everything together.

4 Tip the mixture into the prepared mould, packing it well into
the corners to push out any air bubbles. Bang the mould on your
bench a few times to help the mixture settle.

5 Bring the loose ends of bacon around the mixture. Cover with the
lid of your terrine, or with a tight layer of foil.

6 Transfer the terrine to a deep tray and pour in enough hot water
to come halfway up the sides. Cook for around 1¼ hours, until the
internal core temperature reaches 72°C on a meat thermometer or
when the juices run clear when the terrine is pierced with a skewer.

7 Transfer the terrine to a tray of iced water to cool it down quickly.
Lift the terrine onto a smaller tray and place a board and a weight
on top of the meat. Leave the terrine to cool completely, then
transfer with weights to the refrigerator.

8 Leave for 1–2 days for the flavours to develop. To serve, allow the
terrine to come to room temperature, cut it into thick slices and
serve with crusty bread, mustard and pickles. The terrine will
keep for up to 7 days in the refrigerator.

Serves 6-8

Poultry

MARIA'S ROAST CHICKEN WITH PARSLEY BUTTER
AND CORNBREAD STUFFING

PROSCIUTTO-WRAPPED CHICKEN WITH MUSHROOM SAUCE

POT-ROASTED CHICKEN WITH NORTH AFRICAN SPICES

SPECIAL FRIED CHICKEN WITH SPICY SWEET-AND-SOUR
DIPPING SAUCE

THAI GREEN CHICKEN CURRY

CHICKEN SATAY SKEWERS WITH PEANUT SAUCE

CONFIT DUCK LEG WITH BORLOTTI BRAISE

QUAIL BAKED WITH LARDO, LEMON AND VINE LEAVES

ASIAN-STYLE PIGEON WITH SICHUAN SALT
AND CHILLI DIPPING SAUCE

THERE ARE quite a few misconceptions about the Australian poultry industry. These days, mass-produced chickens and turkeys are not pumped full of hormones and antibiotics, but many of them do live in horrible conditions in order to get them to the table as fast as possible.

The thing is, it takes time (and therefore money) for farmers to raise chickens properly, and that means they are inevitably going to cost the customer more. But morality aside, free-range and organic chooks just do taste loads better. I know that there are lots of people who won't be able to afford a top-notch chook all the time, but even if you only make that choice every now and then, you'll soon discover the difference in quality. I'd even go as far as to say that perhaps it's worth eating meat-free a couple of nights a week, and splashing out on a bloody good chicken as an occasional treat, instead of eating tasteless and inhumanely reared chicken more often.

One of the best tips I can offer with poultry is to buy a whole bird rather than ready-prepared pieces. It's the best way I know to get value for your money as virtually nothing goes into the bin. You can use the breasts for schnitzels, the legs for a curry, and then save and freeze the wings for the barbecue, and use the carcass for a stock or a soup. And if you roast a whole bird for a chicken dinner, the leftover bones make a pretty good stock, too.

MARIA'S ROAST CHICKEN WITH PARSLEY BUTTER AND CORNBREAD STUFFING

My mum, Maria, cooks the best roast chicken in the world. When my brother and I were small, one big chook was enough to feed the family, although we always ended up squabbling over who would get to chew on the bones. When Mum decided to cook two chickens, we never looked back!

The chicken is stuffed under the skin with a herb butter, which keeps the breast meat moist, and inside there's a tasty cornbread stuffing that soaks up all the juices. If there's any extra stuffing mixture, roll it into a sausage shape, wrap it in buttered foil and roast it alongside the chicken.

Combine the ingredients for the parsley butter in a bowl, mixing well. Turn out onto a piece of plastic wrap and roll the butter into a log. Cover with the plastic, twist the ends and refrigerate until required.

To make the stuffing, heat the oil in a heavy-based frying pan and gently fry the onion and garlic for 3–4 minutes, until the onion is soft but not coloured. Transfer to a mixing bowl and allow to cool. Add the corn kernels and remaining ingredients and mix thoroughly. Set aside until ready to use.

Preheat the oven to 180°C. Wipe the cavity of the chicken with paper towel and trim off any excess fat. Hold the chicken firmly with one hand, and with the other, carefully insert your fingers under the skin that covers the breasts. Gradually ease the skin away, being careful not to tear it. Take small knobs of parsley butter and push them under the skin, until butter covers most of the breasts. Pull the skin back in place over the breasts.

Put the stuffing inside the chicken. Firmly tie the legs to the chicken and place the chicken on a wire rack inside a large roasting tray. Season generously with salt and pepper, rub with the oil, and roast for 1–1½ hours, until the internal core temperature reaches 72°C on a meat thermometer or when the juices run clear when you insert a skewer into the thigh.

Leave the chicken to rest in a warm place for 15 minutes while you cook your vegetables and pour yourself a nice glass of wine.

Serves 4

1.5 kg free-range chicken

salt

freshly ground black pepper

1 tablespoon olive oil

Parsley Butter

100 g butter at room temperature

3 tablespoons finely chopped flat-leaf parsley

1 garlic clove, crushed

1 teaspoon salt

1 teaspoon freshly ground black pepper

Cornbread Stuffing

1 tablespoon olive oil

1 onion, finely diced

1 garlic clove, crushed

2 corncobs, boiled, kernels sliced off

½ cup chopped flat-leaf parsley

2 tablespoons chopped thyme

140 g breadcrumbs

100 g butter, melted

1½ teaspoons salt

freshly ground black pepper

PROSCIUTTO-WRAPPED CHICKEN WITH MUSHROOM SAUCE

An elegant chicken dish that is perfect for a low-key dinner party on a chilly autumn evening. I like to serve it with rice pilaf or creamy, buttery mash (page 12), and I always serve it with Nonna's Roman Beans (page 13). For a simpler meal, serve it with some steamed green beans and warm crusty bread to mop up the sauce.

Preheat the oven to 170°C.

Season the chicken breasts all over with salt and pepper and sprinkle with the thyme and sage. Wrap a slice of prosciutto around each breast.

Heat the oil in a large heavy-based frying pan and add 2 breasts, frying until browned all over. Transfer to a medium ovenproof dish and brown the remaining breasts.

Add the shallots to the pan and fry until golden. Add the bacon and fry for a further 3–4 minutes, then tip the mixture into the dish with the chicken.

Melt the butter in the pan until just foaming. Add the garlic and mushrooms and fry gently for 5–6 minutes, until the mushrooms are beginning to soften. Increase the temperature to high and add the wine. Allow it to bubble vigorously for a moment, then add the stock and cream. Return to a boil, then pour over the chicken.

Stir the sauce as best you can to mix the ingredients together. Bake for 20–25 minutes, or until the chicken is cooked through. Sprinkle with parsley before serving.

Serves 4

4 free-range chicken breasts

salt

freshly ground black pepper

1 tablespoon roughly chopped thyme

1 tablespoon roughly chopped sage leaves

4 slices of prosciutto

3 tablespoons olive oil

8 shallots, quartered

100 g bacon, cut into 1 cm strips

75 g butter

2 garlic cloves, crushed

200 g button mushrooms, thickly sliced

150 ml white wine

100 ml chicken stock

400 ml cream

3 tablespoons chopped flat-leaf parsley

POT-ROASTED CHICKEN WITH NORTH AFRICAN SPICES

I love to pot-roast chicken as it keeps the meat wonderfully moist and tender. You can use a whole chook if you prefer, but here I use marylands, which I cut into more manageable pieces through the joint. This recipe is full of exotic spices and the cooking aromas will whisk you away to a Moroccan souk.

Preheat the oven to 180°C. Season the chicken pieces generously with salt and pepper.

Heat half the oil in a large heavy-based frying pan and brown the chicken pieces in batches over medium–high heat. Transfer to a large casserole pot.

Add the rest of the oil to the pan and lower the heat to medium. Fry the onion, garlic and ginger for 3–4 minutes, until the onion is soft but not coloured. Add the chilli and dried spices and fry for another minute, stirring well. Add the stock and bring to a boil. Stir in the olives and fresh herbs. Pour onto the chicken pieces and cover with the lid.

Bake in the oven for 45 minutes. Remove the lid and bake for a further 20 minutes, until the chicken pieces are nicely browned.

Stir in the lemon juice and take to the table to serve.

Serves 4

4 free-range chicken marylands, cut through the joint to separate drumsticks and thighs

salt

freshly ground black pepper

3 tablespoons olive oil

4 medium onions, grated

6 garlic cloves, finely chopped

2 tablespoons grated ginger

2 small red chillies, seeded and finely sliced

2 teaspoons sweet paprika

2 teaspoons cumin seeds, toasted and ground

1 teaspoon coriander seeds, toasted and ground

1 teaspoon saffron threads

500 ml chicken stock

200 g green olives, pitted

2 cups roughly chopped flat-leaf parsley

2 cups roughly chopped coriander leaves

juice of 3 lemons

SPECIAL FRIED CHICKEN WITH SPICY SWEET-AND-SOUR DIPPING SAUCE

I can never go past fried chicken, as I find there is something irresistible about the juicy meat in its crisp, crunchy coating. It's particularly good with this dipping sauce — and perhaps a few icy-cold beers. For maximum flavour, allow the chicken to marinate for at least ten hours, and preferably twenty-four hours. Do take care when deep-frying the chicken; it's not something to do when the kids are with you in the kitchen.

Combine the marinade ingredients in a large mixing bowl. Add the chicken pieces and turn until evenly coated. Cover and refrigerate overnight, or for up to 24 hours, to allow the flavours to develop.

When you are almost ready to cook the chicken, sift the ingredients for the seasoned flour into a mixing bowl and stir well. Lightly beat the egg wash ingredients in another bowl. Whisk the ingredients for the dipping sauce in a serving bowl.

Heat vegetable oil in a deep-fryer or a large saucepan to 180°C. Also preheat the oven to 100°C.

Lift the chicken pieces out of the marinade and let them drain for a few moments. Dip the pieces in the seasoned flour and shake off any excess. Dunk them into the egg wash, then back in the flour again. Deep-fry the chicken pieces in 2 or 3 batches to maintain the temperature of the oil. They will take 6–10 minutes to cook, and should be crisp and golden brown. Briefly drain the fried chicken on paper towel, then transfer to a wire rack set inside a tray and keep warm in the oven while you cook the remaining chicken.

Serve the fried chicken and dipping sauce with lots of paper napkins.

Serves 4–6

1.8 kg free-range chicken, jointed into 12 pieces

vegetable oil for deep-frying

Marinade

2 teaspoons salt

3 tablespoons vinegar (sherry, cider or rice)

1 tablespoon freshly ground white pepper

1 teaspoon grated ginger

1 tablespoon dried chilli flakes

2 garlic cloves, crushed

3 tablespoons roughly chopped coriander leaves

2 tablespoons soy sauce

Seasoned Flour

140 g cornflour

80 g plain flour

40 g self-raising flour

1 tablespoon freshly ground white pepper

1 teaspoon ground cinnamon

1 teaspoon sweet paprika

Egg Wash

3 eggs

500 ml milk

Dipping Sauce

3 tablespoons vinegar (sherry, cider or rice)

3 tablespoons kecap manis

2 tablespoons hoisin sauce

1 small red chilli, seeded and finely chopped

THAI GREEN CHICKEN CURRY

I know you can buy Thai curry pastes everywhere these days. But I still believe it is almost as easy to make your own from scratch — and homemade versions do have a much fresher and more vibrant flavour. If you have a food processor, you can whiz up a curry paste in a matter of minutes. I often make it in large quantities and freeze it to have on hand whenever I need a curry fix!

I cook the curry sauce on its own — which you can even do ahead of time — and add the chicken in thin slices in the last five minutes.

Combine the curry paste ingredients in a food processor and blend to a paste.

Heat the oil in a large heavy-based saucepan. Add the curry paste, lemongrass and lime leaves and fry for 3–5 minutes, stirring, until fragrant. Stir in the palm sugar, then the coconut cream and stock. Bring to a boil, then lower the heat and simmer for 20 minutes, stirring from time to time.

Add the sliced chicken and allow to return to a simmer. Cook for 5–10 minutes, until the chicken is just cooked through. Stir in the lime juice and serve with steamed rice.

Serves 4

3 tablespoons vegetable oil

1 lemongrass stalk, bruised with the back of a knife and cut in half

2 kaffir lime leaves

50 g palm sugar

800 ml coconut cream

500 ml chicken stock or water

800 g free-range chicken breasts, finely sliced

juice of 2 limes

Green Curry Paste

1 onion, finely sliced

4 garlic cloves, crushed

3 tablespoons grated ginger

3 tablespoons grated galangal (optional)

1 small green or red chilli, seeded and sliced

2 cups roughly chopped coriander roots, stalks and leaves

2 tablespoons fish sauce

1 tablespoon soy sauce

CHICKEN SATAY SKEWERS WITH PEANUT SAUCE

I have wonderful childhood memories of the years I spent living on the island of Penang in Malaysia while my dad was in the Australian Air Force. One of the things I remember most is the amazing food — especially the satay skewers, which really are the Malaysian national dish. Every time I grill chicken satays in my back garden, it transports me back to that magical time.

Use wooden skewers for these satays, and don't forget to soak them in water beforehand to prevent them burning.

1 kg free-range chicken thighs or breasts, cut into 3 cm dice

Marinade

3 tablespoons vegetable oil

3 tablespoons soy sauce

1 tablespoon fish sauce

1 tablespoon sesame oil

2 tablespoons dried chilli flakes

4 garlic cloves, crushed

3 tablespoons grated ginger

2 shallots, finely diced

1 cup roughly chopped coriander leaves

juice of 1 lime

Combine the marinade ingredients in a large mixing bowl. Add the chicken pieces and toss until evenly coated. Cover and refrigerate overnight to allow the flavours to develop.

To make the sauce, heat the oil in a small saucepan. Fry the shallots, garlic, ginger, softened chilli flakes, lemongrass and spices for 3–4 minutes, until fragrant. Strain the tamarind water and add it to the pan with the sugar, fish sauce and salt. Stir in the peanuts and simmer gently for about 4–5 minutes, or until the sauce thickens and the oil separates to form a thin layer on the surface. The sauce can be made to this stage in advance.

Remove the chicken from the refrigerator at least 30 minutes before you want to eat. Mix the cucumber and pineapple in a small serving bowl.

Preheat your barbecue grill to low–medium. While it is heating, thread the chicken pieces onto soaked wooden skewers. Cook them for 8–10 minutes, turning frequently to make sure they don't burn.

While the chicken is cooking, gently reheat the peanut sauce. Stir in the coriander and lime juice.

Mound the skewers onto a large platter and serve straight away with the peanut sauce and cucumber and pineapple salad.

Serves 6–8

Peanut Sauce

3 tablespoons vegetable oil

2 shallots, finely sliced

2 garlic cloves, crushed

1 teaspoon grated ginger

3 tablespoons dried chilli flakes, soaked in 3 tablespoons water for 1 hour

$\frac{1}{2}$ lemongrass stalk (split lengthwise), finely sliced and pounded to a paste

1 tablespoon coriander seeds, toasted and ground

1 tablespoon caraway seeds, toasted and ground

3 tablespoons tamarind pulp softened in 750 ml warm water

1 tablespoon brown sugar or grated palm sugar

1 tablespoon fish sauce

1 teaspoon salt

$1\frac{1}{2}$ cups peanuts, roasted and chopped

$\frac{1}{2}$ cup chopped coriander leaves

juice of 1 lime

Salad

1 lebanese cucumber, finely diced

$\frac{1}{2}$ small pineapple, peeled, cored and finely diced

CONFIT DUCK LEG WITH BORLOTTI BRAISE

Confit is a traditional French technique for cooking and preserving meats such as duck, goose or pork in their own rendered fat. In my opinion, it's one of the best things you can do to a duck leg! Confit duck can be stored for up to a month in the refrigerator, as long as it is completely submerged in the fat.

Fresh borlotti beans are plentiful by the cool autumn months, and are immeasurably better than dried or tinned beans. This earthy braise works brilliantly with the crisp richness of the duck.

Combine the salt, pepper, fennel and herbs in a small mixing bowl. Place the duck legs on a plastic tray and rub them all over with the salt mixture. When they are thoroughly salted, cover loosely with plastic wrap and refrigerate overnight.

The next day, rinse away the salt rub and pat the legs dry with paper towel. Heat the duck fat in a large heavy-based saucepan until it just starts to bubble. Slip the legs into the fat one at a time, and return the fat to a gentle simmer. Turn the heat as low as you can and cook the duck for $1\frac{1}{4}$ hours. The meat should be very tender but not yet falling away from the bones. Remove the pan from the heat and leave the duck to cool in the fat. (If you plan to store the confit duck, put the legs in an earthenware dish and ladle on enough fat to cover them completely. Leave to cool, then refrigerate for up to 1 month. Bring to room temperature before using.)

To make the borlotti braise, bring a saucepan of salted water to a boil and cook the beans for 15–20 minutes, until al dente.

Meanwhile, gently heat the oil with the garlic in a separate heavy-based saucepan. Add the onion, bay leaf, thyme and fennel seeds and fry gently for 3–4 minutes, until the onion is soft but not coloured. Add the carrot, celery and fennel and fry for a further 5 minutes. Pour in the wine and bring to a boil. Bubble vigorously for 1 minute, then add the stock and passata. Return to the boil, then lower the heat and simmer for 10–15 minutes.

3 tablespoons salt flakes

1 tablespoon freshly ground black pepper

1 teaspoon fennel seeds, ground

2 tablespoons chopped thyme

2 tablespoons chopped flat-leaf parsley

6 duck legs

1 litre duck fat

Borlotti Braise

1 kg fresh borlotti beans, podded to yield 500 g

3 tablespoons olive oil

3 garlic cloves, finely chopped

1 onion, finely diced

1 bay leaf

2 thyme sprigs

1 teaspoon fennel seeds

1 medium carrot, cut into 1.5 cm dice

2 celery stalks, cut into 1.5 cm dice

1 medium fennel bulb, finely sliced

250 ml white wine

750 ml chicken stock

500 ml Tomato Passata (page 156)

1 medium zucchini, cut into 1.5 cm dice

salt

freshly ground black pepper

1 cup basil leaves

To Serve

extra-virgin olive oil

$\frac{1}{2}$ cup chopped flat-leaf parsley

Drain the beans and add them to the braise with the zucchini. Simmer for 3–5 minutes, or until the beans and vegetables are tender. Season to taste with salt and pepper and keep warm.

Preheat the oven to 180°C.

Sear the confit duck legs, skin-side down in a very hot non-stick frying pan. Turn them over and transfer to a wire rack set in a roasting tray. Bake in the oven for 10 minutes until crisp all over and warmed though.

Fold the basil leaves into the borlotti braise and divide between plates. Arrange a duck leg on top, drizzle with a little extra-virgin olive oil and scatter with parsley.

Serves 6

QUAIL BAKED WITH LARDO, LEMON AND VINE LEAVES

Quite a few Aussie backyards boast a grapevine over the back porch — especially if they belong to an Italian or Greek family. They are not just grown for the grapes, as the vines themselves give welcome shade from the heat, and from spring through to late summer they provide a steady supply of fresh leaves. Vine leaves are probably best known stuffed with rice to make dolmades, but they can also be wrapped around other foods to add flavour and protection against the heat of a barbecue or oven.

In this recipe, the slight lemony flavour of the leaves complements the mildly gamey flavour of quail. I wrap each small bird in a strip of tasty lardo, then in the vine leaf. The birds are infused with wonderful flavour as they roast, and the lardo also keeps the meat moist. Tabbouleh (for recipe see page 37) and Minted Yoghurt (for recipe see page 120) are the perfect accompaniments, along with finger bowls for sticky fingers.

If using fresh vine leaves, blanch them briefly in boiling water. If using preserved leaves — available in jars from delicatessens — you just need to rinse them.

Blanch the vine leaves if using fresh leaves, or rinse them if using preserved. Pat the leaves dry, and cut out the stems.

Preheat the oven to 200°C. Season the quail generously inside and out. Fill the cavity of each bird with a sprig of thyme, a bay leaf and a slice of lemon, and tuck in a piece of butter. Wrap each bird in a slice of lardo (or pancetta) and drizzle with a little oil.

Roll each bird in a vine leaf, then wrap in a large square of foil. Arrange the quail in a baking tray and roast for 20–25 minutes. If you like your quail crisp, you can then open the foil and vine leaf and brown under the grill for 2–3 minutes.

Unwrap the foil (reserving any cooking juices) and carefully remove the vine leaves from the quails. Split the quails in half and serve them with the vine leaves on the side and a drizzle of cooking juices. I like to sit them on smoky Baba Ghanoush (page 111), or serve them with tabbouleh salad and minted yoghurt.

Serves 4

4 fresh or preserved vine leaves

4 jumbo quail

salt

freshly ground black pepper

4 thyme sprigs

4 bay leaves

4 slices of lemon

50 g butter, cut into 4 pieces

4 long slices of Lardo (page 206) or pancetta

2 tablespoons olive oil

ASIAN-STYLE PIGEON WITH SICHUAN SALT AND CHILLI DIPPING SAUCE

I'm not ashamed to confess that I love all deep-fried poultry. This recipe is inspired by the spicy pigeon you find in Chinese restaurants. Pigeon (also known as squab) is particularly suited to deep-frying and its rich, gamey flavour goes brilliantly with this spicy salt and chilli sauce.

Prepare the pigeons by cutting off their heads, necks and claws and cutting them into quarters.

Combine the cornflour, peppers, chilli and salt in a large mixing bowl. Add the pigeon pieces and toss until thoroughly coated.

In separate serving bowls, combine the ingredients for the sichuan salt and the chilli dipping sauce.

Heat the oil in a deep-fryer or a large saucepan to 180°C. Also preheat the oven to 100°C. Deep-fry the pigeon pieces in a few batches to maintain the temperature of the oil. If you like your pigeon rare, as I do, it will need about 5 minutes in the oil and should become a glossy deep brown. It can be cooked longer if you prefer. Briefly drain the fried pigeon on paper towel, then transfer to a wire rack set inside a tray and keep warm in the oven while you cook the remaining pigeon.

Serve the pigeon piping hot with lemon or lime wedges, the sichaun salt and the chilli dipping sauce.

Serves 4

4 pigeons, weighing 450 g each

50 g cornflour

2½ tablespoons ground sichuan pepper

1 tablespoon freshly ground black pepper

1 tablespoon dried chilli flakes or finely chopped fresh chilli

1 teaspoon salt

vegetable oil for deep-frying

lemon or lime wedges to serve

Sichuan Salt

1 teaspoon salt

1 teaspoon ground sichuan pepper

1 teaspoon dried chilli flakes or finely chopped fresh chilli

1 tablespoon chopped coriander leaves

Chilli Dipping Sauce

1 tablespoon finely chopped fresh chilli

3 tablespoons chopped coriander leaves

3 tablespoons soy sauce

2 tablespoons sherry vinegar

juice of 1 lime

Meat

THE PERFECT ROAST BEEF

ROAST BEEF FILLET WITH THYME

POT-ROASTED PORK SHOULDER WITH APPLES,
CABBAGE AND CIDER VINEGAR

ROLLED PORK LOIN WITH CRACKLING

BRAISED LAMB WITH MOROCCAN SPICES

ROLLED LAMB SHOULDER BRAISED WITH EGGPLANT,
ROSEMARY, GARLIC AND HERBS

SLOW-COOKED VEAL WITH GARLIC,
ROSEMARY AND WHITE WINE

LAMB SHANKS WITH MUSHROOMS
AND STICKY PORT GLAZE

RABBIT BRAISED IN GOLDEN ALE

SUNDAY-NIGHT MEATLOAF
WITH SWEET ONION GRAVY

MEXICAN-SPICED SAUSAGES

MERGUEZ SAUSAGES

I KNOW THIS is going to sound a bit strange given my reputation as a meat-lover, but I reckon that we Australians eat far too much of the stuff. And the same can be said for most countries in the wealthy Western world. Not only is the over-consumption bad for our health, but the poor old animals get a raw deal, too, in the way they are intensively reared for our convenience.

In the old days, before large-scale farming, meat was quite expensive, so people ate it in much smaller amounts and less often. The other important difference was that people were much less wasteful. They were dab hands at turning the cheaper cuts, off-cuts and offal into delicious meals. Lots of my butcher mates tell me that they find it really hard to sell the secondary cuts because many people have never heard of them. They only know about the prime cuts, such as steaks and chops and leg or loin roasts. I reckon they don't know what they're missing out on.

I am a firm believer in the 'nose-to-tail' approach to meat, whether it be pork, beef or lamb. I also think we have a duty to give our animals the best possible life. What this means in practice is choosing meat that is free-range at least, or organic at best. That way you know the animal will have been reared more slowly, fed a more varied, less concentrated diet, and will be clear of many growth-enhancing hormones and antibiotics. The upside for us — apart from any benefit to our conscience — is that the meat from these animals tastes so much better. I always say that a happy animal is a tasty animal.

Apart from choosing good-quality, humanely raised meat, I'd like to encourage you to branch out and try some of the lesser known cuts. You'll find recipes in this chapter for using the shank, neck and shoulder, all economical cuts that are transformed by slow cooking into delicious and tender meals.

8.10
11.80
19.90

THE PERFECT ROAST BEEF

A standing rib of beef is a splendid cut. In my book, there's nothing to beat it at any time of the year — but it's especially good for a mid-winter feast.

A standing rib is the equivalent of a rack of lamb — but so much more impressive — and it has a thick layer of creamy surface fat that protects the meat from the heat of the oven. During the cooking, the fat renders out and keeps the meat lovely and moist. The meat itself is marbled with more fat, which adds loads of flavour from the inside out.

Ask your butcher to remove the feather bones at the base, but to leave the covering of fat on your roast. I like to score the fat deeply and rub in plenty of salt and pepper so that it becomes crisp and golden.

Serve your roast with all the trimmings, but above all, don't forget the horseradish cream. Made from freshly grated horseradish and sour cream, it is far superior to anything you can buy in a jar.

Preheat the oven to 220°C.

With a very sharp knife, score deep incisions into the surface fat of the roast. Toss the salt and pepper with the thyme and rub the mixture all over the beef, working it into the fat and meat. Sit the beef on a wire rack inside a large roasting tray. Roast for 8 minutes to brown the meat all over, then lower the temperature to 160°C and roast for 35–40 minutes, until the internal core temperature reaches 45°C on a meat thermometer, indicating the meat is cooked medium–rare.

Remove the roast from the oven, cover with foil and leave to rest for 30 minutes in a warm place.

To make the horseradish cream, mix the horseradish with the vinegar. Fold in the sour cream and chives. Season to taste. (The cream will keep in the refrigerator for up to 2 days.)

If the roast has cooled too much for your liking, you can reheat it in the oven for 4–5 minutes. Transfer to a warm serving plate and take to the table to carve and serve.

Serves 6–8

3 kg standing rib roast, feather bones removed

3 tablespoons salt

2 tablespoons freshly ground black pepper

2 tablespoons chopped thyme

Horseradish Cream

100 g horseradish root, peeled and grated

2 tablespoons white wine vinegar

350 ml sour cream

2 tablespoons finely snipped chives

salt

freshly ground black pepper

ROAST BEEF FILLET WITH THYME

Beef fillet is always a good choice for special occasions. In fact, it's the perfect cut for a dinner party or buffet table as it looks beautiful and you can cut it into neat, even slices. The most important thing to remember is not to overcook it, and to let it rest for a decent length of time. Serve it with hot English mustard and roasted root vegetables (try the Roast Vegetables with Rosemary and Garlic and Feta Dressing on page 18).

Preheat the oven to 180°C. Tuck the thin tail-end of the fillet underneath so that the beef is an even thickness all along its length. Tie securely with butcher's string at 5 cm intervals. Smear a thin coating of oil all over the beef, season with salt and pepper, and rub on the thyme.

Heat a few tablespoons of oil in a heavy-based frying pan. When it is very hot, brown the beef fillet all over. Transfer to a wire rack inside a roasting tray and roast for 12–15 minutes, or until the internal core temperature reaches 38°C on a meat thermometer, indicating the beef is cooked rare. (If you prefer your beef cooked longer, 45°C indicates medium–rare, 55°C medium and 65°C medium–well done.) Keep in mind that the temperature will continue rising by about 5°C once you take the meat from the oven.

When the beef is cooked to your liking, cover with foil and leave to rest for at least 10 minutes in a warm place.

To serve, snip away the string and carve the beef into thick slices. Serve with hot English mustard and roasted vegetables.

Serves 6

1.4 kg eye-fillet of beef

olive oil

1 teaspoon salt

1 tablespoon freshly ground black pepper

3 tablespoons roughly chopped thyme

hot English mustard to serve

POT-ROASTED PORK SHOULDER WITH APPLES, CABBAGE AND CIDER VINEGAR

Pork shoulder is a really rewarding cut. It's made up of several different muscles, which means the meat is layered with lots of fatty connective tissue that breaks down during long, slow cooking to create a lovely tender meal. Serve with buttered new potatoes or hunks of crusty bread.

Ask your butcher for a boned and rolled shoulder with the skin left on. That way you can crisp it up at the end of the cooking time.

Preheat the oven to 150°C. Open out the pork shoulder and lay it skin-side down on your work surface. Rub 1 teaspoon of the salt along with the pepper and herbs into the meat, then roll the shoulder up and tie securely with butcher's string at 3 cm intervals. You can prepare the pork to this stage up to 2 days in advance — the herbs and seasoning will permeate the flesh and add extra flavour.

To make the braise, melt the butter in an ovenproof pot. Add the onion, garlic, fennel seeds, thyme and bay leaf and fry gently for 3–4 minutes, until the onion is soft but not coloured. Add the celery, carrot, cabbage, cloves and cinnamon stick and cook for a further 3–4 minutes. Stir in the apple, vinegar, wine and stock and remove from the heat.

Rub the pork skin with the oil, then the rest of the salt. Transfer the pork to the pot and cover with the lid. Cook for 1½ hours, or until the meat is very tender and falling apart.

Increase the oven temperature to 200°C and take the lid off the pot. Cook for a further 30–40 minutes to crisp and brown the skin of the pork. If necessary, add a little water to the pot to keep the braise nice and wet.

Remove from the oven, cover the pork with foil and leave to rest for 20 minutes in a warm place. Lift the pork out of the pot, carve into thick slices and lay onto plates. Stir the parsley into the braise and spoon over the pork.

Serves 4–6

1.5 kg boned and rolled pork shoulder with skin

2 tablespoons salt

1 tablespoon freshly ground black pepper

¼ cup sage leaves

3 tablespoons chopped thyme

100 ml olive oil

Apple, Cabbage and Vinegar Braise

100 g butter

1 medium onion, finely diced

4 garlic cloves, crushed

1 teaspoon fennel seeds

3 tablespoons chopped thyme

1 bay leaf

1 celery stalk, cut into 2 cm dice

2 medium carrots, cut into 2 cm dice

¼ cabbage, cut into rough 3 cm squares

2 cloves

1 cinnamon stick

6 granny smith apples, peeled, cored and cut into 2 cm dice

250 ml apple cider vinegar

250 ml white wine

500 ml chicken stock

½ cup roughly chopped flat-leaf parsley

ROLLED PORK LOIN WITH CRACKLING

Is there anyone who doesn't love crackling? Not in my family! I always think the loin is a great dish to serve up to lots of people (and big families) as it's so easy to slice. And you can easily make sure that everyone gets the same amount of crackling so there won't be any fighting.

Ask your butcher to keep enough of the belly flap to wrap the meat into a roll. Pork always goes brilliantly with braised cabbage, but for a change serve it with Brussels Sprouts with Bacon and Garlic Butter (page 12). For a condiment, try mustard or Apple, Currant and Cinnamon Relish (page 174).

Lay the pork skin-side down on your work surface. Rub half the salt and all the pepper into the meat, then scatter on the garlic and herbs. Roll the loin up into a long log and tie securely with butcher's string at 3 cm intervals. You can prepare the pork to this stage up to 2 days in advance — the garlic and herbs will permeate the flesh and add extra flavour.

Preheat the oven to 220°C and place the pork on a rack inside a large roasting tray. Rub all over with the oil, then with the rest of the salt. Roast for 20 minutes, then lower the temperature to 175°C and roast for a further hour, or until the internal core temperature reaches 72°C on a meat thermometer.

Cover the pork with foil and leave to rest for 30 minutes in a warm place. If the meat has cooled too much for your liking after resting, you can reheat it in the oven for 4–5 minutes.

Remove the string and carve the pork into slices, each with a crisp layer of crackling.

Serves 8–12

2.5 kg boned pork loin for rolling, with skin

2 tablespoons salt

1 tablespoon freshly ground black pepper

3 garlic cloves, finely sliced

½ cup flat-leaf parsley leaves

¼ cup sage leaves

3 tablespoons chopped thyme

125 ml olive oil

BRAISED LAMB WITH MOROCCAN SPICES

This wonderful slow-cooked lamb dish is full of exotic spices — it's a great introduction to the flavours of North Africa and perfect for those who don't like chilli heat. Serve it with a big bowl of fluffy couscous and with Minted Yoghurt (for recipe see page 120).

Season the lamb pieces generously with salt and pepper. Combine the onion, carrot, ginger and garlic in a food processor and blitz to a puree.

Preheat the oven to 160°C.

Heat the oil in an ovenproof pot and brown the lamb pieces all over. Transfer to a plate, then add the carrot puree to the pot and cook for 4–5 minutes over low heat. Add the spices and bay leaves and cook for a further 5 minutes. Stir in the coriander and stock and bring to a boil.

Return the lamb to the pot along with the currants, pine nuts and pistachios. Cover with the lid and bake for $2\frac{1}{2}$–3 hours, until the lamb is very tender and falling apart.

Stir in the lemon juice, honey, parsley and mint. Serve garnished with the flaked almonds and coriander leaves.

Serves 6

2 kg leg of lamb, boned and cut into 6 even chunks

salt

freshly ground black pepper

2 onions, roughly chopped

2 large carrots, roughly chopped

100 g ginger, peeled and roughly chopped

6 garlic cloves

3 tablespoons olive oil

1 tablespoon cumin seeds, toasted and ground

1 tablespoon coriander seeds, toasted and ground

1 teaspoon ground allspice

6 cloves

4 cardamom pods, roughly crushed

1 cinnamon stick

2 bay leaves

2 cups roughly chopped coriander leaves, plus extra leaves to garnish

1 litre chicken stock

120 g currants

120 g pine nuts

60 g pistachios

juice of 2 lemons

3 tablespoons honey

1 cup roughly chopped flat-leaf parsley

1 cup roughly chopped mint

2 tablespoons flaked almonds, toasted, to garnish

ROLLED LAMB SHOULDER BRAISED WITH EGGPLANT, ROSEMARY, GARLIC AND HERBS

To my way of thinking, the forequarter or shoulder of lamb is one of the very best parts, albeit not as popular as the leg. It is perfectly suited to long, slow cooking, when it becomes meltingly soft and tender. In this wintery braise, the eggplant cooks down to a thick sauce, and all you'll need by way of accompaniment is some warm crusty bread.

When you ask your butcher for a boned lamb shoulder, ask for the bones as well (and get him to cut them for you). Then, you can make your own wonderful lamb stock for braising the lamb.

Preheat the oven to 160°C. Open out the lamb shoulder on your work surface. Season the meat with salt and pepper, then rub with the lemon zest, thyme and oregano, half the rosemary and a quarter of the garlic. Roll the shoulder up into a fat log and tie securely with butcher's string at 3 cm intervals.

Heat the oil in a pot and brown the lamb shoulder all over. Transfer to a plate. Add the onion, fennel seeds and remaining rosemary and garlic to the pot and fry gently for 3–4 minutes, until the onion is soft but not coloured. Add the celery and carrot and fry for 2–3 minutes. Add the eggplant and fry for a further 4–5 minutes, stirring from time to time.

Return the lamb to the pot and pour in the wine and stock. The meat should be just about submerged in the liquid. Bring to a boil, then lower the heat and simmer, covered, for $2\frac{1}{2}$–3 hours.

Before serving, stir in the lemon juice and parsley.

Serves 6

1.4 kg boned lamb shoulder for rolling

salt

freshly ground black pepper

grated zest of $\frac{1}{2}$ lemon

2 tablespoons roughly chopped thyme

1 teaspoon dried oregano

$\frac{1}{3}$ cup roughly chopped rosemary leaves

8 garlic cloves, crushed

125 ml olive oil

2 medium onions, finely diced

1 teaspoon fennel seeds

2 celery stalks, cut into 1 cm slices

2 large carrots, cut into 1 cm slices

2 large eggplants, cut into 2 cm dice

500 ml white wine

1 litre lamb or chicken stock

juice of 2 lemons

$\frac{1}{2}$ cup roughly chopped flat-leaf parsley

SLOW-COOKED VEAL WITH GARLIC, ROSEMARY AND WHITE WINE

Most people, if they are at all familiar with veal, only know it as schnitzels. I think it's well worth learning how to cook the secondary cuts such as the shoulder and shank, as they have a deeper flavour and are less expensive. The Italians, of course, know how to make the best of all cuts of veal.

This is a recipe for braised veal shoulder on the bone, which keeps the meat juicy. It is perfect served with soft polenta.

Preheat the oven to 165°C. Season the veal pieces with salt and pepper.

Heat the oil in an ovenproof pot and brown the veal pieces all over. Transfer to a plate.

Lower the heat under the pot and add the butter, onion, garlic, rosemary and bay leaves and fry for 3–4 minutes, until the onion is soft but not coloured. Add the celery and carrot and cook for a further 3–4 minutes.

Return the veal pieces to the casserole and pour on the wine and chicken stock. Bring to the boil, then cover the casserole and cook in the oven for 1 hour. Remove the lid and cook for a further 30 minutes, uncovered, by which time the meat should be very tender and falling from the bone.

Before serving, stir in the lemon juice and parsley.

Serves 6

1.5 kg veal shoulder, cut through the bone into 6 pieces

salt

freshly ground black pepper

3 tablespoons olive oil

100 g butter

2 onions, cut into 2 cm dice

20 garlic cloves, sliced in half

$\frac{1}{2}$ cup loosely packed rosemary leaves

2 bay leaves

2 celery stalks, cut into 2 cm dice

2 large carrots, cut into 2 cm slices

500 ml white wine

375 ml chicken stock

juice of 1 lemon

$\frac{1}{2}$ cup roughly chopped flat-leaf parsley

LAMB SHANKS WITH MUSHROOMS AND STICKY PORT GLAZE

The times when lamb shanks were a cheap-and-cheerful cut have long gone. These days it seems that everyone knows how delicious they are and they are priced accordingly. But in my book they are worth every cent! The mushrooms and port wine in this recipe really bring out the underlying sweetness of the shanks. The only thing you need is a big bowl of buttery mashed potatoes (page 12).

Preheat the oven to 160°C. Season the lamb shanks with salt and pepper.

Heat the oil in an ovenproof pot and brown the shanks all over. Transfer to a plate.

Lower the heat under the pot and add the butter, onion, garlic, thyme and bay leaf and fry for 3–4 minutes, until the onion is soft but not coloured. Add the mushrooms and stock and bring to a boil. Simmer for 10 minutes, until the mushrooms are soft. Add the port and return to the boil.

Return the lamb shanks to the pot, making sure they are completely submerged in the sauce. Season with more salt and pepper, cover with the lid and bake for 2 hours, by which time the meat should be very tender and falling from the bone.

Increase the oven temperature to 200°C, remove the lid and cook for a further 30–40 minutes, until the sauce reduces and thickens. Keep an eye on it to make sure it doesn't burn.

Serve with lots of mashed potatoes.

Serves 4

4 lamb shanks (shanks from the hind legs are meatier)

salt

freshly ground black pepper

3 tablespoons olive oil

100 g butter

2 onions, finely sliced

6 garlic cloves, crushed

2 tablespoons roughly chopped thyme

1 bay leaf

500 g mushrooms (mixed varieties if possible), sliced 1 cm thick

375 ml chicken stock

375 ml port

RABBIT BRAISED IN GOLDEN ALE

I love rabbit's mild yet distinctive flavour — and I love beer! So what could be better than combining the two? Sometimes I cook this dish until the rabbit is really tender, then I pull all the meat off the bones and serve it as a sauce with fluffy little pillows of Potato Gnocchi (page 286). But it is just as good served in chunks on the bone with a big bowl of mash (page 12).

350 ml golden ale (or other beer of your choice)

2 teaspoons chopped thyme

1 teaspoon roughly chopped rosemary leaves

2 bay leaves

1.2 kg rabbit, jointed

salt

freshly ground black pepper

2 tablespoons olive oil

100 g butter

1 medium onion, finely diced

5 garlic cloves, crushed

2 celery stalks, cut into 2 cm dice

2 carrots, cut into 2 cm dice

1 litre chicken stock

$\frac{1}{2}$ cup chopped flat-leaf parsley

Mix the beer, thyme, rosemary and bay leaves in a large mixing bowl. Add the rabbit pieces and toss until evenly coated. Cover and refrigerate for at least 1 hour, or up to overnight, to allow the flavours to develop.

Remove the rabbit from the marinade, pat dry and season with salt and freshly ground black pepper. Reserve the marinade.

Preheat the oven to 165°C. Heat the oil in an ovenproof pot and brown the rabbit pieces all over, then transfer to a plate.

Lower the heat under the pot and add the butter, onion and garlic and fry for 3–4 minutes, until the onion is soft but not coloured. Add the celery and carrot and cook for a further 3–4 minutes.

Return the rabbit pieces to the pot and pour on the chicken stock and reserved marinade. Bring to a boil, then bake without a lid for 1$\frac{1}{2}$ hours, by which time the meat should be very tender and falling from the bone. Stir in the parsley and serve with mashed potatoes.

Serves 4

SUNDAY-NIGHT MEATLOAF WITH SWEET ONION GRAVY

This is a real favourite in my house, and somehow we always seem to eat it on a Sunday. We love it with mashed potatoes and peas, and the next day we love the leftovers even a bit more, in sandwiches (the kids' with tomato relish and mine with a big dollop of chilli sauce, mayonnaise and hot mustard).

Preheat the oven to 180°C and lightly oil a loaf tin.

Combine all the ingredients in a large mixing bowl, using your hands to squish everything together thoroughly.

Spoon the mixture into the tin and bake for 1 hour, or until cooked through. If it looks to be browning too quickly, cover with foil.

When the meatloaf is cooked, turn it out onto a warm serving plate. Tip the excess fat and juices into a small frying pan to use for the gravy. Set the pan over medium–high heat and add the butter. When it foams, add the onion, garlic and thyme and cook for 3–4 minutes, until the onion is soft but not coloured. Add the stock and bring to a boil. Add the cornflour and simmer for another 3 minutes, then add the parsley and remove from the heat.

Slice the warm meatloaf thickly and serve with mashed potatoes, peas and plenty of sweet onion gravy.

Serves 6

1 kg minced chuck or blade beef

500 g minced pork neck

60 g diced bacon

1 onion, finely diced

2 garlic cloves, crushed

5 eggs, 3 hardboiled and roughly chopped, 2 lightly beaten

140 g breadcrumbs

125 ml red wine

3 tablespoons mustard

2 tablespoons kecap manis (Indonesian sweet soy sauce) or soy sauce

1 tablespoon chopped thyme

1 tablespoon chopped flat-leaf parsley

1 tablespoon salt

1 tablespoon freshly ground black pepper

Gravy

100 g butter

4 onions, very finely sliced

2 garlic cloves, crushed

2 thyme sprigs

375 ml good-quality chicken stock

1 tablespoon cornflour mixed with a little water

1 tablespoon chopped flat-leaf parsley

Masterclass

HOW TO MAKE SAUSAGES

juice of 1 lemon

1.5 metres natural sausage casings
— but buy double in case of tears

800 g pork neck, chilled

250 g pork back fat, chilled

50 g fennel seeds

½ cup chopped flat-leaf parsley

1 tablespoon freshly ground white
pepper

1 tablespoon salt

1 teaspoon dried chilli flakes
(optional)

NOTE

*These are classic pork and fennel
sausages. Other ingredients that
work really well in sausages include
peppers, fresh herbs, spices, red
wine and garlic. So feel free to
experiment though bear in mind
that simple combinations often
work best.*

1 Fill a bowl with lukewarm water and stir in the lemon juice. Soak the sausage casing for 10–15 minutes.

2 With a very sharp knife, trim away any tendons, sinew or bits of bone from the pork neck and discard. Cut the meat into 2 cm dice. Slice the skin away from the back fat and discard. Cut the fat into 2 cm dice.

3 Combine the diced meat and fat in a large mixing bowl.

4 Finely grind half the fennel seeds, then add the ground and whole seeds and remaining ingredients to the meat.

5 Use your hands to mix everything together well.

6 Push the mixture through a mincer fitted with a 6 mm plate.

7 Fix a sausage-making attachment to the mincer. Carefully ease the entire length of casing over the nozzle, leaving about 6 cm dangling. Tie a knot in the end of the casing.

8 Pack the mouth of the mincer with sausage meat, being careful not to trap any air.

9 Hold the casing in the palm of one hand and turn the mincer's handle with the other. Maintain a steady rhythm so the casing fills smoothly and evenly right down to the knotted end. Add more sausage meat to the mincer when needed.

CONTINUED »

10   When the casing is filled to within 6 cm of the end, detach it from the mincer and tie a knot to seal.

11   Lay the sausage on your work surface and, if necessary, use your hands to roll it gently to distribute the filling evenly.

12   Twist the sausage a complete turn at even intervals to create individual sausages. (Twist each sausage the opposite way to the last to prevent them unwinding.) Tie butcher's string around each join. Refrigerate the link of sausages at least overnight before cooking. They will keep for up to 4 days in the refrigerator, or up to 3 months in the freezer.

Makes 6–8 sausages

MEXICAN-SPICED SAUSAGES

I've been to Mexico a few times and have always really loved the people, the place and the food. I reckon Mexican cooking is very underrated; it is quite simple, but really fresh and tasty. They eat lots of fruit, vegetables and salads, and heaps of herbs and spices. Chilli features, of course. But in Mexico there are literally hundreds of varieties: fresh, dried, smoked, hot and mild.

These sausages are quite spicy, but are perfect for warming you up on a cold winter's day. See page 264 for extra tips on making sausages.

Fill a bowl with lukewarm water and stir in the lemon juice. Soak the sausage casing for 10–15 minutes.

With a very sharp knife, trim away any tendons, sinew or bits of bone from the pork neck and discard. Slice the skin away from the back fat and discard. Cut the pork neck and back fat into 2 cm dice.

Put the meat and fat in a large mixing bowl and add the remaining ingredients. Use your hands to mix everything together well.

Push the mixture through a mincer fitted with a 6 mm plate.

Carefully ease the length of casing over the mincer's sausage-making attachment, leaving about 6 cm dangling at the end. Attach it to the mincer. Pack the mincer with sausage meat, being careful not to trap any air. Fill the sausage casing. Twist to form individual sausages and tie the joins with butcher's string. Refrigerate the link of sausages at least overnight before cooking (they can be stored for up to 4 days).

Cook the sausages in a frying pan or on a barbecue. Serve in a crusty bun with Tomato Relish (for recipe see page 177) and a good chilli sauce.

Makes 6–8

juice of 1 lemon

1.5 metres natural sausage casings — but buy double in case of tears

800 g pork neck, chilled

200 g pork back fat, chilled

1 tablespoon salt

1 tablespoon cumin seeds, toasted and ground

100 g fresh jalapeño chillies, seeded and finely chopped

2 tablespoons tomato paste

½ cup roughly chopped coriander leaves

1 teaspoon smoked paprika

1 tablespoon freshly ground black pepper

1 tablespoon dried oregano

MERGUEZ SAUSAGES

Merguez are spicy North African sausages that are often cooked in tagines and served with couscous and hot harissa paste. They are made from beef or mutton and are sometimes a little lean for my liking, so when I make them at home or for my restaurant, I usually add some pork back fat to the mixture.

I like to wrap these sausages in caul fat, which keeps them moist but melts away as they cook (you may need to give your butcher some notice to get caul fat). However, the sausages can also be made the traditional way, stuffed into a natural casing (see page 264).

With a very sharp knife, trim away any tendons, sinew or bits of bone from the beef and lamb and discard. Slice the skin away from the back fat and discard. Cut the beef, lamb and back fat into 2 cm dice.

Combine the meat and remaining ingredients except for the caul fat in a large mixing bowl. Use your hands to mix everything together well.

Push the mixture through a mincer fitted with a 6 mm plate. Divide the sausage mixture into 8 portions and roll each one into a fat sausage.

Cut the caul fat into 8 rectangles slightly longer and about twice the width of the sausages. Wrap each piece tightly around a sausage. Refrigerate the sausages at least overnight.

Cook the sausages in a frying pan for 8–10 minutes, or until cooked through. Serve with Minted Yoghurt (for recipe see page 120), a good spicy relish and plenty of flatbread.

Makes 8

600 g lean beef, chilled

300 g lamb shoulder or leg meat, chilled

200 g pork back fat, chilled

2 tablespoons sweet paprika

1 tablespoon hot paprika

1 teaspoon dried chilli flakes

1 teaspoon cumin seeds, toasted and ground

1 teaspoon ground allspice

$\frac{1}{2}$ teaspoon ground cinnamon

2 cloves, ground

1 cup chopped coriander leaves

3 garlic cloves, crushed

1 tablespoon salt

2 teaspoons dried mint

120 g currants

200 g caul fat, rinsed

Pasta

LINGUINE WITH CARAMELISED ONIONS,
GARLIC, CHILLI AND PARSLEY

NONNA'S VEAL RAVIOLI

PENNE AL FORNO

LINGUINE WITH CLAMS

SPAGHETTI WITH MEATBALLS

RICOTTA GNOCCHI WITH CHIVE BUTTER AND PEAS

ASK AROUND, and I reckon you'll find nearly all your friends eat pasta at least a couple of times every week. I grew up eating pasta every single day, and I still think it's the food of the gods.

But there's pasta and there's pasta. As with so many things in life, you get what you pay for. Expensive dried pasta doesn't cost more just because of the fancy packaging. It's actually a better, tastier product, and I reckon it's worth paying a bit more for it. I also encourage people to move out of their comfort zone and buy different pasta shapes. Whenever I go to my local Italian deli, I swear I always find a shape I've never seen before.

I think it's worth learning how to make your own fresh pasta, too. You won't want to do it all the time, but when you've had a go at making pasta yourself, you'll realise that it's in a completely different league. Have a look at the Masterclass on page 274 and give it a go. It's also an easy way to get kids involved in the kitchen.

One final word about pasta: when it comes to the cheese that goes on top, whatever you do, avoid the pre-grated, sawdust kind. You don't need to be precious about always buying a pricy parmigiano reggiano — a locally made parmesan will do, as long as you grate it fresh at every meal.

Masterclass

HOW TO MAKE FRESH PASTA

6 eggs (58 g each)
8 egg yolks (from 58 g eggs)
1 tablespoon extra-vigin olive oil
800 g plain flour
1 teaspoon salt

1 Combine the eggs and yolks in a mixing bowl and whisk together lightly.

2 Sift the flour and salt into a mound on a large work surface. Form a wide, deep well in the centre and carefully pour in the eggs.

3 Use a fork to gradually work the flour into the eggs, being careful not to let the eggs spill out.

4 When enough flour has been incorporated into the eggs that they hold shape, use your hands to work in all the remaining flour to form a dough.

5 Scrape the work surface clean and wash and dry your hands. Place the dough on the clean surface and knead it firmly but without too heavy a hand. Sprinkle the dough with a little more flour if it feels very sticky, but don't allow it to become dry.

6 Knead steadily for 5–6 minutes, turning regularly, or until smooth and elastic. Cover with plastic wrap and leave to rest at room temperature for 30 minutes.

CONTINUED »

7   When ready to roll, divide the dough into quarters and shape each piece into a flat rectangle.

8   Working with one piece at a time, pass it through the widest setting on a pasta machine, then turn it ninety degrees and pass it through again.

9   Decrease the setting by a notch and pass the dough through twice (without turning). Continue to roll the dough through the machine once on each following setting until you reach the desired thickness. For cut pastas, such as fettucine or linguine, finish one notch before the final setting. For stuffed pastas, such as ravioli, work through to the thinnest setting.

10   Roll the sheets through the cutters to create your desired pasta. Or if using the dough for stuffed pasta, proceed immediately without letting the dough dry out. Cook the pasta in plenty of salted boiling water.

Makes 1 kg

LINGUINE WITH CARAMELISED ONIONS, GARLIC, CHILLI AND PARSLEY

This is one of my favorite winter pasta dishes. Slicing the large amount of onions will give your arms a workout, but they melt down to a wonderful golden sweetness. Throw in the garlic, chilli and parsley and it will knock any winter sniffles on the head.

Heat the oil in a large heavy-based saucepan. Add a third of the sliced onions and stir over medium–high heat for 5-6 minutes, until softened and starting to colour. Add the remaining onions and stir them in thoroughly. Lower the heat a little and cook for around 20 minutes, until the onions have softened and coloured a lovely golden brown.

Meanwhile, cook the linguine in a pot of boiling salted water until al dente.

Add the garlic, chilli, anchovies and olives to the onions and stir for 4–5 minutes, by which time the mixture should smell irresistible! Season sparingly with salt and pepper (the anchovies and olives are already salty).

Drain the pasta well and toss with the caramelised onion mixture. Fold in the parsley and serve with lashings of parmesan.

Serves 4

250 ml olive oil

5 large onions, finely sliced

400 g dried linguine

8 garlic cloves, crushed

1 chilli, finely sliced (hot or mild, according to taste)

2 anchovy fillets

150 g kalamata olives, pitted and left whole

salt

freshly ground black pepper

2 cups roughly chopped flat-leaf parsley

freshly grated parmesan to serve

NONNA'S VEAL RAVIOLI

I grew up on veal ravioli, as it was one of my nonna's specialities. It *always* featured at the dinner table on Christmas Day. You definitely need a lot of time to make it — Nonna used to take all day making the veal stuffing and homemade pasta — but the results are well worth the effort.

You can roll the pasta out by hand, but I really recommend buying a pasta machine. They are inexpensive and easy to use, and they last a lifetime.

This recipe makes around eighty to ninety pieces of ravioli, enough to serve six to eight people as a main course. If you don't eat veal, you can make this with yearling beef or pork instead.

Heat the oil in a heavy-based saucepan and brown the piece of veal all over. Transfer to a plate. Melt the butter in the pan, then add the onion, garlic and anchovy and cook over low heat for 3–4 minutes, until the onion is soft but not coloured. Increase the heat and stir in the port. Let it bubble vigorously for a few minutes, then stir in the basil and tomato passata. Return the veal to the pan and bring to a simmer. Cook for about 2 hours, uncovered, until the veal is very tender. The sauce will become very thick and intense in flavour, but if it seems to be sticking to the bottom of the pan, add a little water. When cooked, remove from the heat and leave to cool.

When cool, remove the veal from the sauce and cut it into thin slices. Reserve the sauce for serving with the ravioli. Put the veal into a food processor with the parsley and parmesan and blend to a fairly smooth puree. Season with salt and pepper.

Roll the pasta dough as described on page 274, finishing with very thin sheets. Cut them into long strips about 5 cm wide. Place spoonfuls of the filling along a pasta strip about 4 cm apart. Brush around the fillings with a little water and cover with another pasta strip. Press gently around the fillings to remove any air and seal. Cut into ravioli with a cutting wheel or a sharp knife. Continue making ravioli until you have used all the dough and filling.

The ravioli should be cooked straight away (or frozen on trays lined with baking paper). Cook in a pot of boiling salted water for 6–8 minutes, or until the ravioli rise to the top of the water. Serve with the warmed tomato sauce and extra parmesan.

Serves 6–8

1 kg Fresh Pasta Dough (page 274)
freshly grated parmesan to serve

Veal Stuffing
2 tablespoons olive oil
800 g veal or yearling beef girello
100 g butter
1 onion, finely diced
4 garlic cloves, chopped
1 anchovy fillet
250 ml port or red wine
$\frac{1}{2}$ cup basil leaves
1.5 litres Tomato Passata (for recipe see page 156)
3 tablespoons chopped flat-leaf parsley
60 g parmesan, grated
salt
freshly ground black pepper

PENNE AL FORNO

Like many Italians, I have been eating *penne al forno* — 'penne baked in the oven' — for as long as I can remember. My nonna, mother and godmother are all experts at making it, and whenever I cook it they take great pleasure in telling me where I've gone wrong! And to be honest, their versions do always seem to taste better than mine!

There are a few stages to preparing *penne al forno*, but none of them are hard. You can make it ahead of time, and it tastes even better the next day. It even tastes delicious cold. The basic recipe can be varied endlessly using whatever vegetables or cheese you have to hand, or even adding meat sauce, which turns it into a kind of cheat's lasagne. There are just a couple of tips to remember: first, boil the penne for half the recommended cooking time as it will continue to absorb liquid and cook in the oven; second, make sure you bake it until the top is golden and crunchy.

To make the bechamel sauce, pour the milk into a saucepan and slowly heat it. Meanwhile, melt the butter in a large heavy-based saucepan. Add the onion, garlic and bay leaf and cook over low heat for 3–4 minutes, until the onion is soft but not coloured. Add the flour and cook, stirring, for 3–4 minutes. Stir in a cup of hot milk at a time, ensuring that each is fully incorporated and lump-free before adding the next. Once all the milk is added, simmer for 5–10 minutes, stirring regularly. Stir in the parmesan and season to taste.

500 g dried penne

2 eggs, lightly beaten

200 g fresh ricotta, crumbled

150 g parmesan, grated

1 cup basil leaves

salt

freshly ground black pepper

Bechamel Sauce

1 litre milk

100 g butter

1 onion, very finely diced

1 garlic clove, crushed

1 bay leaf

100 g plain flour

100 g parmesan, grated

salt

freshly ground black pepper

Tomato Sauce

100 g butter

1 large onion, finely diced

2 garlic cloves, crushed

½ cup basil leaves

1 litre Tomato Passata (for recipe see page 156)

salt

freshly ground black pepper

To make the tomato sauce, heat the butter in a large heavy-based saucepan. Fry the onion, garlic and basil for 3–4 minutes, until the onion is soft but not coloured. Add the tomato passata and bring to a boil. Lower the heat and simmer gently for 15 minutes, then season to taste with salt and pepper.

When ready to assemble, preheat the oven to 180°C. Cook the penne in a large saucepan of boiling water for half the recommended cooking time. Drain well, then tip the half-cooked pasta into a large mixing bowl with the eggs, ricotta, half the parmesan and all the basil. Add a quarter of the bechamel sauce and three-quarters of the tomato sauce and mix everything together well. Season to taste with salt and pepper. Tip into a 25 x 40 cm baking dish, then spread the rest of the tomato sauce over the surface. Cover with the remaining bechamel sauce and sprinkle on the remaining parmesan. Bake for 45–60 minutes, until the surface is golden and crunchy. Serve with a green leaf salad.

Serves 6–8

LINGUINE WITH CLAMS

When my brother and I went on family holidays down the coast of Port Phillip Bay, we used to collect small clams from the waterfront. We'd take them back to our beach house and my nonna used them to make the classic Italian dish, *linguine alla vongole*. Sadly, it's illegal to remove clams from the bay now, but every now and then, when my own kids dig them up, I tell them about the good old days and my nonna's famous dish. And then, of course, I have to cook up a big pot of it in her memory.

The clams you buy from the fishmonger are usually pretty clean, but you may occasionally find a little sand inside the shells. For this reason, some people like to cook the clams first and then remove them from the shells before mixing them into the pasta. But I prefer to toss everything together, shells and all, as my nonna did.

125 ml extra-virgin olive oil, plus extra to serve

1 red onion, finely sliced

6 garlic cloves, crushed

1 long red chilli, finely sliced

400 g dried linguine

2 kg vongole clams, rinsed

1 cup chopped flat-leaf parsley

salt

freshly ground black pepper

Heat the oil in a large heavy-based saucepan. Add the onion, garlic and chilli and cook over low heat for 5–10 minutes, until the onion is very soft but not coloured.

Meanwhile, cook the linguine in a pot of boiling salted water until al dente.

While the linguine is cooking, add the clams to the saucepan with the onion, garlic and chilli. Cover with the lid and turn the heat up high. Cook for 2–3 minutes, shaking the pan fairly vigorously from time to time. Take off the lid and check the clams, discarding any that have refused to open.

Drain the linguine well, then add to the saucepan with the clams. Add the parsley and season lightly with salt and pepper. Toss well, then divide between bowls and serve with drizzles of extra-virgin olive oil.

Serves 4

SPAGHETTI WITH MEATBALLS

My boys love spaghetti and meatballs — I think all kids do. This recipe includes a secret ingredient: a big dollop of kecap manis — Indonesian sweet soy sauce — which you'll find in most supermarkets.

To make the meatballs, combine all the ingredients except the oil in a large mixing bowl. Use your hands to squish everything together thoroughly. Cover and refrigerate for 20 minutes to allow the flavours to develop.

To make the sauce, heat the butter and oil in a large heavy-based saucepan. Gently fry the onion, garlic and basil for 3–4 minutes, until soft but not coloured. Add the tomato passata and bring to a boil. Lower the heat and simmer gently for 20 minutes, then season to taste with salt and pepper.

Meanwhile, divide the meatball mixture into walnut-sized pieces and roll into smooth, round balls. Heat a little olive oil in a heavy-based frying pan and fry the meatballs in batches until evenly browned. Add them to the tomato sauce and simmer for around 30 minutes.

Cook the spaghetti in a pot of boiling salted water until al dente. Drain well and return to the pot. Stir in the butter and parsley and season lightly with salt and pepper. Add a ladle of meatball sauce and toss well. Divide the spaghetti between serving bowls and top with meatballs and extra sauce. Serve with plenty of parmesan.

Serves 4–6

500 g dried spaghetti

20 g butter

$\frac{1}{2}$ cup chopped flat-leaf parsley

salt

freshly ground black pepper

freshly grated parmesan to serve

Meatballs

500 g minced chuck or blade beef

500 g minced pork neck

3 garlic cloves, crushed

2 tablespoons kecap manis (Indonesian sweet soy sauce)

$\frac{1}{2}$ cup chopped flat-leaf parsley

$\frac{1}{4}$ cup grated parmesan

140 g breadcrumbs

salt

freshly ground black pepper

olive oil

Tomato Sauce

50 g butter

$2\frac{1}{2}$ tablespoons olive oil

1 large onion, finely diced

3 garlic cloves, crushed

1 cup basil leaves

2 litres Tomato Passata (page 156)

salt

freshly ground black pepper

Masterclass

HOW TO MAKE POTATO GNOCCHI

1 kg nicola potatoes (or any
variety of yellow waxy potato)

salt

250 g plain flour,
plus extra for dusting

1 egg

parmesan to serve

1 Place the potatoes in a large saucepan of cold salted water. Bring to the boil, then lower the heat and simmer until tender — this can take up to 50 minutes, depending on the size of the potatoes.

2 Drain the potatoes and peel them when cool enough to handle.

3 Bring 2 litres of salted water to a boil, ready to cook the gnocchi.

4 Lightly dust a work surface with flour. Push the potatoes through a food mill or potato ricer directly onto the surface.

5 Sprinkle with a little salt and sift on the flour. Crack the egg straight onto the flour and use your hands to work the flour and egg into the potato as gently and quickly as you can, until just combined. The dough should be light and slightly springy.

6 Divide the dough into 6 pieces. Roll into long cigars and cut into 3 cm lengths. Use the back of a fork to imprint the characteristic gnocchi ridges.

7 Adjust the temperature under the pot of water to give you a gentle rolling boil. Drop in a third of the gnocchi, a few at a time, stirring very gently as you do so to keep the water moving.

8 The gnocchi should rise to the surface within 1–2 minutes, indicating they are cooked. Lift them out with a slotted spoon and transfer to a warm, lightly buttered dish while you cook the remaining gnocchi.

9 Serve with your choice of sauce and lots of grated parmesan.

Serves 6

RICOTTA GNOCCHI WITH CHIVE BUTTER AND PEAS

Ricotta gnocchi are a breeze to make, but are best if you use good-quality fresh ricotta from a delicatessen or Italian food store, rather than the mass-produced stuff you find in the supermarket. I serve the gnocchi with a simple chive-butter sauce so as not to overpower the mild, fresh flavour.

The quantity of flour you need will vary depending on the ricotta. I recommend you add three-quarters of the flour, then the rest a little at a time, just until the mixture holds together.

Bring a pot of salted water to a boil, ready to cook the gnocchi.

Combine the ricotta, parmesan and egg in a large mixing bowl and lightly mash them all together. Sift on three-quarters of the flour and use your hands to mix it in gently. Add more, as required, until the dough just holds together. It should be very soft.

Divide the dough into 3 pieces and place on a lightly floured work surface. Roll the pieces into long cigars and cut into 2 cm lengths. Handle the gnocchi gently as they will be quite fragile.

To make the sauce, melt the butter in a large heavy-based frying pan. Add the garlic and fry gently for 3–4 minutes, then stir in the peas, chives and parsley. Season with salt and pepper and keep over a very low heat while you cook the gnocchi.

Adjust the temperature under the pot of water to give you a gentle rolling boil. Drop in half of the gnocchi, a few at a time, stirring very gently as you do so to keep the water moving. After about 3–4 minutes they will rise to the surface, indicating they are cooked. Lift them out with a slotted spoon and transfer to the frying pan while you cook the remaining gnocchi.

Gently toss all the gnocchi in the sauce and serve straight away with grated parmesan.

Serves 4

500 g fresh ricotta, mashed with a fork

100 g parmesan, grated, plus extra to serve

1 egg, lightly beaten

150 g plain flour

150 g butter

1 garlic clove, crushed

1 cup peas, blanched

3 tablespoons snipped chives

2 tablespoons chopped flat-leaf parsley

salt

freshly ground black pepper

Pies

STEAK AND BACON PIES FOR THE FOOTY

CHICKEN, MUSHROOM AND LEMONY LEEK PIES

SILVERBEET, CURRANT AND PINE NUT PIE

CURRIED BEEF AND CHUNKY VEG PIES

RHUBARB, APPLE AND GINGER CRUMBLE

CHERRY PIE

APPLE TARTE TATIN

FOR ME,

a pie should have a crisp, golden, flaky pastry, and a rich, flavoursome filling. I want a pie that crunches when I bite into it, that fills my kitchen with wonderful aromas. I want a pie that delights all my senses, so for me, there's no question that homemade is best. And the good news is that pies are really, really easy to make.

Pies are the complete package, and they are also perfect portable food. And the varieties — both savoury and sweet — are endless! You can knock up a pie from a leftover casserole and a sheet of good-quality frozen pastry, or you can create a filling from scratch and be as creative as you like.

STEAK AND BACON PIES FOR THE FOOTY

My boys are finally old enough to take to footy matches — I'm talking Australian Rules football, not soccer — and I'm doing my best to make sure they support the right team!

The good old Aussie meat pie is a footy tradition, but I'd rather my kids ate pies I've made at home than the miserable ones you can buy at the game. This is their favourite. The pies are really sturdy and won't fall apart, and we always make sure we take along plenty of tomato sauce or Tomato Relish (for recipe see page 177) to dollop on top.

The pastry is easy to make and bakes to a lovely golden crispness. It uses suet, which you can buy from your butcher. It can be stored in the freezer for up to three months and you can use it straight from the freezer, as it's easier to grate.

To make the filling, heat the oil in a large heavy-based saucepan. Brown the beef in batches over medium–high heat, then transfer to a plate. Fry the bacon until golden and transfer to the same plate.

Add the butter to the pan and lower the heat. Add the onion and garlic and fry for 3–4 minutes, until the onion is soft but not coloured. Add the carrot and cook for 3–4 minutes. Return the beef and bacon to the pan and add the sauces and stock. Bring to a boil, then lower the heat and simmer uncovered for 1 hour, or until the beef is very tender. Add the cornflour and simmer for another 3 minutes (the mixture should become nice and thick), then add the parsley and remove from the heat. Leave to cool.

Meanwhile, make the pastry. Grate the suet onto a work surface and sift on about 100 g of the flour. Use a large, sharp knife to chop the suet with the flour (this prevents the suet from becoming sticky).

Transfer the suet to a large mixing bowl and sift on the remaining flour and salt. Use your fingertips to rub the suet into the flour, but leave it a little rough and lumpy as this helps the pastry to rise.

Suet Pastry

350 g frozen suet

700 g plain flour

1 teaspoon salt

400 ml cold water

Filling

2 tablespoons olive oil

1 kg rump or blade steak, cut into 2 cm dice

200 g thick-cut smoked bacon or kaiserfleisch, cut into 1 cm dice

2 tablespoons butter

2 onions, finely diced

3 garlic cloves, crushed

1 large carrot, grated

1 tablespoon worcestershire sauce

3 tablespoons tomato sauce

1.5 litres chicken or beef stock

40 g cornflour mixed with a little water

½ cup chopped flat-leaf parsley

Egg Wash

2 egg yolks

80 ml milk

Add the water a little at a time until the mixture just comes together (you may not need all of the water). Transfer the dough to your work surface and knead for 2–3 minutes, until elastic and springy. Cover in plastic wrap and refrigerate for at least 30 minutes.

Preheat the oven to 200°C and lightly grease 6 x 12 cm pie tins. Roll out the pastry on a lightly floured work surface to around 5 mm thick. Cut 6 circles large enough to line the tins with a 2 cm overhang. Lay the pastry into the tins. Spoon the filling into the pies to three-quarters full. Re-roll the remaining pastry and cut out 6 smaller circles to form the lids.

Lightly beat the egg yolks and milk to make the egg wash. Brush the rims of the pies with egg wash and place the lids on top. Press firmly around the edges to seal the pies, then roll the rolling pin over the top of the pie to trim away any excess pastry. Make a small slit in the lids so steam can escape as the pies bake. Brush the tops with egg wash and bake the pies for 20–25 minutes, or until the pastry is cooked on the underside and the tops are a lovely golden brown. Remove from the oven and eat straight away, or leave to cool a little before wrapping in foil to take to the footy.

Makes 6 pies

CHICKEN, MUSHROOM AND LEMONY LEEK PIES

This is a classic chicken and mushroom pie with a bit of a twist — the lemon thyme adds a subtle lemon flavour.

When I make chicken pies, I prefer to use chicken thighs on the bone and roast the meat in the oven as I think the meat is more tender and the flavour much better than breasts. But you can use boneless thighs or breasts if you prefer. As for the pastry, by all means use a good-quality purchased puff pastry, but I really believe that once you've tasted your own homemade rough puff, shop-bought stuff just won't suffice.

This recipe is for individual pies but you could make one large family-sized pie if you prefer.

The recipe here makes about one kilogram of pastry and you will need less than five-hundred gram for these pies. But it's well worth making the larger amount and freezing the rest to have handy for future use.

To make the pastry, combine the butter, flour and salt in a mixing bowl. Use your fingertips to rub the butter into the flour, but leave it a little lumpy rather than rubbing to uniform sandy crumbs. Add the water a little at a time (you may not need all of it) and work it into the flour mixture until it just comes together as a dough. You should still be able to see little flecks of butter in the pastry. Cover in plastic wrap and refrigerate for 1 hour.

Roll the pastry out on a lightly floured work surface to a long rectangle of about 20 x 40 cm, and 5 mm thick. Fold the ends in over each other to make 3 layers. Roll it out to another long rectangle the same dimensions as before and fold it into thirds again. Cover in plastic wrap and refrigerate for 30 minutes.

Rough Puff Pastry

500 g unsalted butter at room temperature, diced

500 g plain flour, sifted

pinch of salt

375 ml cold water

Filling

6 large skinless chicken thighs on the bone (around 1.2 kg)

salt

freshly ground black pepper

2 tablespoons chopped lemon thyme

3 tablespoons oil

100 g butter

1 large onion, finely diced

4 garlic cloves, crushed

2 celery stalks, finely sliced

1 medium leek, finely sliced

1 bay leaf

300 g mushrooms, finely sliced

500 ml chicken stock

50 g cornflour mixed with a little water

½ cup chopped flat-leaf parsley

2 tablespoons chopped dill

100 ml cream

Egg Wash

2 egg yolks

80 ml milk

Do another round of rolls and folds, then refrigerate for another 30 minutes. The pastry is now ready to use. Set aside 500 g for the pies (if you are not using it immediately, you can wrap it tightly in plastic wrap and store it in the refrigerator for up to 4 days). Freeze the rest for another occasion, for up to 3 months.

To make the filling, preheat the oven to 180°C. Season the chicken thighs with salt and pepper and sprinkle on a little of the lemon thyme. Heat the oil in a heavy-based frying pan and brown the thighs all over. Transfer to an oven tray and bake for 20 minutes, or until the chicken comes away from the bone easily. Leave to cool, then take the meat from the bones. Cut into 3 cm chunks and set aside.

Melt the butter in a heavy-based saucepan and add the onion, garlic, celery, leek, bay leaf and half the remaining lemon thyme. Cook for 3–4 minutes, until soft but not coloured. Add the mushrooms and cook for a further 5 minutes, until tender. Add the stock and bring to a boil, then lower the heat and simmer for 5 minutes. Add the cornflour amd simmer for another 3 minutes, then add the parsley, dill and remaining lemon thyme. Remove from the heat, stir in the cream and season with salt and pepper.

Preheat the oven to 200°C. Divide the chicken pieces evenly between 6 x 12 cm pie dishes, then spoon over the sauce.

Lightly beat the egg yolks and milk to make the egg wash. On a lightly floured work surface, roll out 500 g of the pastry to around 5 mm thick. Cut out 6 circles large enough to cover the pie dishes, leaving a small overhang. The remnants can be re-rolled, wrapped in plastic wrap and used for another dish. Lightly brush the rims of the dishes with a little egg wash and place the lids on top. Press the pastry to the rims to seal, then roll the rolling pin over the top of the pies to trim off any excess pastry. Make a small slit in the lids so steam can escape as the pies bake. Brush each pie with egg wash and bake for 15–20 minutes, until the tops have puffed up to a lovely golden brown.

Makes 6 pies

SILVERBEET, CURRANT AND PINE NUT PIE

If there is one vegetable that everyone seems to be able to grow, it is silverbeet. In my garden it goes crazy and I'm always looking for delicious new ways to cook it. This Middle Eastern pie is a little bit exotic and always a crowd-pleaser. It uses crisp filo pastry, readily available from supermarkets.

Cut the silverbeet leaves from the stems. Slice the stems into 1 cm pieces and roughly chop the leaves.

Melt half the butter in a large heavy-based frying pan. Add the onion and garlic and fry gently for 3–4 minutes, until the onion is soft but not coloured. Add the ginger and silverbeet stems and cook for 5 minutes, until the stems are beginning to soften. Add the silverbeet leaves and stir well over the heat for another 5 minutes until they are completely wilted.

Stir in the cinnamon, currants and pine nuts, then the cream, feta, parsley and lemon juice. Remove the pan from the heat and leave to cool for a few minutes before stirring in the eggs, salt and pepper.

Preheat the oven to 200°C. Melt the rest of the butter and lightly brush some inside a 20 x 22 cm baking dish. Lay a sheet of filo into the dish and brush with more butter. Top with 4 more sheets, brushing with butter as you go. Now spoon in the silverbeet filling and spread it out evenly. Top with the remaining sheets of pastry, brushing each with butter. Fold in the edges of the pie and brush the top and edges with butter. Bake for 25–30 minutes, until golden brown. Serve hot or at room temperature with a garden salad.

Serves 6

1 kg silverbeet
200 g butter
1 large onion, finely diced
3 garlic cloves, crushed
1 teaspoon grated ginger
½ teaspoon ground cinnamon
120 g currants
80 g pine nuts
100 ml cream
100 g feta, crumbled
½ cup chopped flat-leaf parsley
juice of 1 lemon
4 eggs, lightly beaten
½ teaspoon salt
1 teaspoon freshly ground black pepper
10 sheets of filo pastry

CURRIED BEEF AND CHUNKY VEG PIES

When I make curried beef pies, I always add some homemade spice mix to the filling as I think it freshens the flavour. Garam masala is an all-purpose Indian spice mix — it's worth making it in a decent quantity as it keeps well in an airtight jar for a few months.

To make the garam masala, put the ingredients in a spice grinder and grind to a fine powder. Alternatively, use a mortar and pestle. Transfer to a jar and store in a cool, dark place.

To make the pie filling, heat the oil in a large heavy-based frying pan. Add the garlic, ginger, curry powder or paste and 1 tablespoon of garam masala. Fry gently for 3–4 minutes until fragrant. Add the onion and cook for a further 3–4 minutes, stirring well. Increase the heat and add the minced beef, stirring for a few minutes to break up any lumps. When the beef is lightly browned, stir in the stock, followed by the carrot and pumpkin. Bring to a simmer and cook for 4 minutes, then add the celery and peas. Simmer for 15–20 minutes, until reduced and thickened, then stir in the salt, coriander and parsley and remove from the heat.

When ready to bake the pies, preheat the oven to 200°C. Spoon the filling into 6 x 12 cm pie dishes. Lightly beat the egg yolks and milk to make an egg wash.

On a lightly floured work surface, roll out 500 g of the pastry to around 5 mm thick. Cut out 6 circles large enough to cover the pie dishes, leaving a small overhang. The remnants can be re-rolled, wrapped in plastic wrap and used for another dish. Lightly brush the rims of the dishes with a little egg wash and place the pastry circles on top. Press the pastry to the rims to seal, then roll the rolling pin over the top of the pies to trim off any excess pastry. Make a small slit in the lids so steam can escape as the pies bake. Brush each pie with egg wash and bake for 15–20 minutes, until the tops have puffed up to a lovely golden brown.

Makes 6 pies

3 tablespoons olive oil

2 garlic cloves, crushed

1 tablespoon grated ginger

3 tablespoons good-quality curry powder or paste

2 onions, finely diced

1 kg good-quality minced beef

250 ml chicken stock

2 large carrots, cut into 1 cm slices

150 g pumpkin, peeled and cut into 2 cm dice

2 celery stalks, cut into 1 cm slices

60 g fresh or frozen peas

2 teaspoons salt

$\frac{1}{2}$ cup chopped coriander

$\frac{1}{2}$ cup chopped flat-leaf parsley

2 egg yolks

80 ml milk

500 g Rough Puff Pastry (for recipe see page 296)

Garam Masala

125 g coriander seeds, toasted

60 g cumin seeds, toasted

60 g black peppercorns

60 g cardamom seeds

30 g cloves

25 g ground cinnamon

$\frac{1}{2}$ teaspoon ground nutmeg

RHUBARB, APPLE AND GINGER CRUMBLE

OK, so technically this is not a pie, but like most people, I love crumble. This combination of rhubarb, apple and spicy fresh ginger is a winner. Serve with custard, thick cream or vanilla ice cream.

Preheat the oven to 180°C. Combine the fruit filling ingredients in a large mixing bowl and toss together thoroughly. Tip into a baking dish.

Combine the crumble ingredients in a food processor and pulse to form rough crumbs. Scatter evenly over the fruit. Bake for 45–60 minutes, until the fruit is bubbling and the crumble is a crunchy golden brown.

Serves 6–8

1 kg rhubarb, cut into 2 cm chunks

6 apples, peeled, cored, and cut into 2 cm chunks

80 g icing sugar

80 g brown sugar

2 tablespoons grated ginger

1 teaspoon ground cinnamon

grated zest of $\frac{1}{2}$ lemon

Crumble Topping

200 g plain flour

100 g rolled oats

75 g brown sugar

150 g unsalted butter at room temperature, diced

pinch of ground nutmeg

pinch of ground cinnamon

75 g almond meal

CHERRY PIE

I make this tart with home-preserved cherries for a touch of summer fruitiness on a chilly winter's day. You can make it with good-quality purchased bottled or tinned cherries – or with fresh cherries, of course.

To make the pastry, mix 2 of the eggs with the egg yolks, vanilla extract and the lemon zest and juice. Reserve the third egg to make an egg wash later on.

Combine the butter and caster sugar in the bowl of an electric mixer and beat until very pale and creamy. Add the egg mixture, a little at a time, beating thoroughly after each addition. Sift on the flour and salt and beat slowly until the mixture just comes together as a ball. It is important not to overmix, or the pastry will be tough. Shape the pastry into a round and wrap in plastic wrap. Refrigerate for at least 1 hour before using.

When ready to blind-bake the tart shell, preheat the oven to 170°C and grease a 28 cm loose-bottomed tart tin. Separate out a third of the pastry and reserve in the refrigerator for making the lattice top. Roll out the rest of the pastry on a lightly floured work surface to about 0.5 cm thickness. Lift the pastry onto the prepared tart tin, easing it in to the edges. Refrigerate for 20 minutes.

Line the pastry with foil and fill with pastry weights (or use rice or dried beans) and bake for 20 minutes. Remove the foil and weights, prick the base of the tart with a fork and return to the oven for 8 minutes. Lightly beat the remaining egg and brush the pastry case lightly. Set aside the rest of the egg wash for later. Return the tart to the oven for 2 minutes to seal. Remove from the oven, trim the edges evenly, if necessary, and set aside.

Roll out the reserved pastry to 0.5 cm thickness. Use a pastry cutter or a sharp knife to to cut into 1 cm strips. Cover with a tea towel while you prepare the filling.

Combine the cherries, raspberries, lemon zest and juice and icing sugar in a large mixing bowl. Toss together very gently, to avoid breaking up the fruit. Tip into a colander to drain away any excess liquid. Mix gently with the cornflour then pile the fruit into the prepared tart shell.

Weave the pastry strips across the top of the tart to form a lattice. Brush the pastry with the reserved egg wash then sprinkle with brown sugar. Bake for 20 minutes, or until the pastry is golden. Allow to cool in the tin for 5 minutes, then remove carefully.

Serves 8

3 eggs

2 egg yolks

2 teaspoons vanilla extract

finely grated zest and juice of 1 lemon

400 g unsalted butter, at room temperature

200 g caster sugar

600 g plain flour

pinch of salt

brown sugar for sprinkling

Filling

1.6 kg bottled cherries (or 4 x 400 g tins pitted cherries or 2 kg fresh cherries, pitted)

300 g raspberries

finely grated zest and juice of 1 lemon

100 g icing sugar, sifted

50 g cornflour

APPLE TARTE TATIN

Sometimes the best recipes come about by accident, as this French tart demonstrates. The name comes from the Tatin sisters who conjured it up in the 1800s from an unintentionally upturned pan of caramelised apples; it is, essentially, an upside-down apple tart. It has become a universal favourite and is equally delicious hot or cold, with ice cream or whipped cream. I sometimes drizzle on a little calvados (apple brandy) at the last minute.

Do take care when you invert the tart onto a plate to serve. It's a good idea to let it cool a little first so you don't get splattered with hot, runny caramel.

To make the pastry, combine the flour, sugar, butter and egg yolks in a food processor and process until the mixture forms a ball of dough. Turn it out onto a work surface and shape into a disc. Cover in plastic wrap and refrigerate for at least 1 hour before rolling.

Melt the butter in a heavy-based ovenproof frying pan around 24 cm in diameter. Add the sugar and stir over medium heat until dissolved. Increase the heat to medium–high and cook for 8–10 minutes to a golden caramel. Carefully add the apple pieces to the pan (the caramel may splutter and spit) and cook for a further 8 minutes, or until the apples have softened but are not mushy. The apples will release their juices and stop the caramel from burning.

While the apples are cooking, preheat the oven to 180°C and roll the pastry out to a circle slightly larger than the frying pan.

Arrange the cooked apples tidily in the pan. Cover with the pastry, tucking the edges into the pan. Bake for 20–25 minutes, or until the pastry is golden brown.

Remove from the oven and allow to cool for 15 minutes or so. To serve, invert the tart onto a plate, drizzle with calvados (if using) and serve with ice cream or whipped cream.

Serves 6–8

150 g unsalted butter

250 g caster sugar

5 granny smith apples, peeled, quartered and cored

calvados to serve (optional)

Pastry

300 g plain flour

80 g caster sugar

250 g unsalted butter at room temperature, diced

2 egg yolks

Puddings

PORTUGUESE PUDDING

RAISIN BREAD-AND-BUTTER PUDDING

CARAMELISED PEAR CAKE

STICKY COFFEE PUDDINGS
WITH CHOCOLATE AND PRUNES

PORTUGUESE PUDDING

I created this pudding as a way of using up sponge cake surplus and it has become one of the bestselling winter desserts on our restaurant menu. (You can bake the sponge a few days in advance, and instead of the berry sauce, the pudding can be made with other pureed fruit, jam or even fig paste.)

To make the sponge, preheat the oven to 170°C. Butter a 27 cm cake tin and line the base and sides with baking paper.

Beat the egg whites to thick, stiff peaks and set aside.

Beat the egg yolks, sugar and vanilla seeds until very pale, thick and creamy. Add the warm melted butter and sift on the flour, but do not stir yet. Now add a third of the egg whites and use a whisk to fold everything together gently but thoroughly. Fold in the rest of the egg whites.

Gently spoon the batter into the prepared tin and bake for 40–45 minutes, or until a skewer comes out clean. Allow the cake to cool in the tin for a few minutes, then invert onto a wire rack and leave to cool completely.

To make the Portuguese custard, whisk the ingredients together until thoroughly combined.

To make the blackberry sauce, combine the ingredients in a saucepan. Cook over low heat for 10–15 minutes, or until the berries begin to disintegrate. Taste and adjust the sweetness to your liking. Leave to cool for 5 minutes, then blitz to a smooth puree in a food processor. While still warm, push the puree through a fine sieve to remove any seeds.

Lightly butter a 30 x 24 x 5 cm baking dish (or use 12 x 170 ml ramekins or terracotta dishes). Cut the sponge cake into small dice. Spread an even layer of blackberry sauce over the base of the dish. Scatter on a loose layer of sponge cake. Pour on enough custard to cover the sponge, then drizzle more blackberry sauce on top. Add another layer of sponge, filling in any gaps. Cover with more custard and drizzle on more blackberry sauce. Add another layer of sponge, then finish with custard. Set aside for at least 1 hour to allow the cake to soak up the custard.

Preheat the oven to 170°C. Bake the pudding for 15–20 minutes, until the surface is golden brown and crisp. Serve with vanilla ice cream or thick cream.

Serves 8–10

Sponge Cake

10 eggs, separated

300 g caster sugar

seeds of 1 vanilla pod

150 g unsalted butter, melted

250 g self-raising flour

Portuguese Egg Custard

500 ml cream

7 egg yolks

$\frac{1}{2}$ cup caster sugar

seeds of $\frac{1}{2}$ vanilla pod

Blackberry Sauce

1 kg fresh or frozen blackberries

200 g caster sugar

juice of 1 lemon

RAISIN BREAD-AND-BUTTER PUDDING

One of the best things about bread-and-butter pudding is that you can make it in so many different ways. You can use plain white bread, fruit bread or panettone, brioche or even croissants, and each pudding is delicious in its own way. This recipe is a Richardson family favourite combining raisin bread and white bread. Crusts on or off? You decide.

Butter a large, deep ovenproof dish and sprinkle it with the caster sugar.

Butter all the slices of bread. If the slices are large, cut them in half diagonally. Arrange the bread slices in the dish in alternating, overlapping layers. Sprinkle with the raisins as you go.

Combine the cream, milk, eggs, brown sugar, cinnamon and vanilla in a large jug or bowl and mix well. Pour over the bread, giving it time to soak in. You may need to do this in a few goes. Set aside for 1 hour to allow the bread to soak up the custard.

Preheat the oven to 175°C. Cover the pudding with foil and bake for 30 minutes. Remove the foil and bake for a further 30 minutes, until the custard has set and the top is golden and crisp. Serve with lots of cold, thick cream.

Serves 6–8

2 tablespoons caster sugar

unsalted butter

1 small loaf of raisin bread, cut into medium-thick slices

1 small loaf of white bread, cut into medium-thick slices

$\frac{1}{2}$ cup raisins

600 ml cream

600 ml milk

6 eggs, lightly beaten

100 g brown sugar

1 teaspoon ground cinnamon

1 teaspoon vanilla extract

CARAMELISED PEAR CAKE

Winter is the peak season for pears and they combine brilliantly with caramel in this moist, tender cake. I like to make it in a kugelhopf tin as it looks very impressive.

Combine the diced pears and brandy or rum in a bowl and set aside.

Thoroughly butter a kugelhopf tin. Cut strips of baking paper about 10 cm wide and lay them around the base of the tin, aiming to cover the base and reach a short way up the sides. This will prevent the pears from sticking to the tin.

To make the caramelised pears, melt the butter in a large heavy-based frying pan. Add the sugar and stir over medium heat until dissolved. Increase the heat to medium–high and cook for 8–10 minutes to a golden caramel. Carefully add the pear quarters (the caramel may splutter and spit) and cook for 10–12 minutes, tossing the pan gently to coat the pears in caramel — they will release their juices and stop the caramel from burning. Remove the pan from the heat and leave to cool for a few moments. Lift the pears out of the caramel and arrange them overlapping around the base of the tin. Reserve the caramel.

Preheat the oven to 160°C. To make the cake, beat the eggs and sugar until pale, thick and creamy. Sift on the flour and baking powder, then fold them into the eggs. Drizzle on the melted butter and fold it in. Gently fold in the diced pears and alcohol.

Spoon the batter into the tin to cover the caramelised pears, then drizzle the reserved caramel over the top. Bake for 40 minutes, or until a skewer comes out clean.

Allow the cake to cool in the tin for 5–10 minutes, then invert it onto a wire rack and leave to cool completely. Carefully peel away the baking paper. Serve the cake on its own or with thick cream.

Serves 8–10

2 pears, peeled, cored and cut into small dice

2 tablespoons brandy or rum

3 eggs

120 g caster sugar

160 g plain flour

1 tablespoon baking powder

140 g unsalted butter, melted

Caramelised Pears

120 g unsalted butter

400 g caster sugar

5 pears, peeled, quartered and cored

STICKY COFFEE PUDDINGS WITH CHOCOLATE AND PRUNES

Dark chocolate and prunes are a marriage made in heaven. Even people who think they don't like prunes will love them in this sticky pud. The coffee and Frangelico work some kind of magic that seems to make the chocolate flavour even more intense.

You can make this as one large pudding in a baking dish, or as small individual puddings, which is what I do here; they are perfect for a dinner party.

Combine 100 g of the prunes and the Frangelico in a small bowl and leave to macerate. Put the rest of the prunes in a saucepan with the coffee and water and bring to a simmer. Cook for 10–15 minutes, or until the prunes are very soft and breaking down. Remove from the heat and stir in the bicarbonate of soda. Leave to cool.

Preheat the oven to 150°C and butter 12 x 120 ml ramekins.

Cream the butter and sugar until the sugar dissolves and the mixture is fluffy. Beat in the eggs one at a time, then stir in the cooled coffee and prune mixture. Fold in the flour, then the chocolate and macerated prunes with any juices. Divide the mixture between the ramekins and bake for 35–40 minutes.

While the puddings are baking, prepare the chocolate sauce. Put the cream in a small saucepan and bring to a boil. Remove from the heat and stir in the chocolate until it melts and you have a smooth sauce.

Serve the hot puddings with the hot chocolate sauce and plenty of cold, thick cream.

Makes 12 puddings

400 g pitted prunes, chopped

80 ml Frangelico

300 ml strong coffee

600 ml water

1 teaspoon bicarbonate of soda

75 g unsalted butter

150 g brown sugar

2 eggs

150 g self-raising flour

200 g good-quality dark chocolate, chopped

Chocolate Sauce

250 ml cream

375 g good-quality dark chocolate, chopped

There are so many people to thank. All of their hard work, long hours, support, encouragement, dedication and loyalty has helped to make my life that much more productive, easier and, most importantly, fun! Thank you all so very, very much!

My family have always been there for me. Their love, devotion and understanding allow me to keep doing the things I love most: being a husband, father and chef.

To my darling Michelle and our three boys: you keep my feet firmly grounded. I could not imagine life without you.

Thanks to Mum, John, Mark and Andrew. And to Dad: you are sadly missed.

To my hard working crew at La Luna Bistro: you are all amazing.

Lynda Horton, my restaurant manager, for so many years of loyal and dedicated hard work, long hours and always smiling, thank you.

My head chef, again, Michael Slade: it's a grind but you love it.

Thanks to Kristy Stewart, for testing and testing.

Lucia, Liana and the rest of the crew out front and back, thank you all so much.

Mary, Ellie and all the Pan Macmillan crew, you guys put so much into this book and boy does it show. Well done!

John and Chris: wow what great pics, no one does shadow like you guys, except for the stylin' shadow himself, Simon. Lovely work, guys.

Suzy, what a design. You took an idea and created a fantastic book, thanks.

Lucy 'you're the best' Malouf, you make a huge task a quick walk in the park, once again, thank you.

Finally, a big thanks to Justine May, the voice of reason. I know how hard you work, thank you!

A Plum book
First published in 2011 by
Pan Macmillan Australia Pty Limited
Level 25, 1 Market Street,
Sydney, NSW 2000, Australia

Level 1, 15–19 Claremont Street,
South Yarra, Victoria 3141, Australia

Written by Adrian Richardson with Lucy Malouf
Design and art direction by Suzy Tuxen at A Friend Of Mine
Typeset by Pauline Haas
Edited by Rachel Pitts
Index by Lucy Malouf
Photography by John Laurie
Props and food styling by Simon Bajada
Food preparation by Kristy Stewart
Colour reproduction by Splitting Image, Clayton, Victoria
Typeset in 20/30 pt Berber King Caps and 9.5/13 pt Miller Display
Handwritten headings by Suzy Tuxen at A Friend of Mine

Printed and bound in China by 1010 Printing International Limited

A CIP catalogue record for this book is available from the National
Library of Australia.

The publisher would like to thank the following for their generosity in providing
props and locations for the book: CERES Organic Market, Izzi & Popo, Major &
Tom, Parks Victoria – Yarra Bend Park, Shelley Panton Ceramics, Step Back Antiques
and The Works – Bed Bath n' Table.

10 9 8 7 6 5 4 3 2